WEBER'S
SMOKE™

BY JAMIE PURVIANCE

PHOTOGRAPHY BY TIM TURNER

FROM THE AUTHOR

Anything smoked used to make my head swim. My confusion really started in rural Louisiana about 30 years ago, when I was a college kid on a summer road trip. One hot and humid afternoon, seductive aromas of wood-smoked pork drifted in my open car window and so, like the true carnivore I am, I followed their path to some county fairgrounds where a barbecue competition was under way. Walking among the teams of brawny cooks and their billowing barbecue rigs, including some rigs that were bigger than my car and probably twice as expensive, I wondered if I might have stumbled into a peculiar cooking cult. What exactly were these people doing with animal carcasses, foot-long meat injectors, wheelbarrows full of wood, and sauces bubbling in battered pots?

Some of the barbecue teams were selling samples, so I paid a dollar for a single sparerib. What I got was a kaleidoscope of tastes that revolved around rich, moist pork deeply nuanced with the fragrance of wood, but what in the world were all those other flavors, and how did the cooks get the succulent meat to slip so easily off the bone? There was so much I didn't know. I just remember making involuntary sighs of appreciation and, even before I was halfway through the first rib, I asked for more.

Years went by and I continued to enjoy good barbecue and other smoked foods on occasion. I learned a fair amount about home cooking along the way, but I assumed that the intricacies of smoked foods were still about as accessible to me as sorcery. It wasn't until I enrolled in a professional cooking school that I finally began to cut through the mystery.

It turns out that man has been smoking foods for thousands of years. It all started as a primitive way of preserving meats so they would not spoil in the hot sun, and it actually hasn't changed much since then. But our reasons for smoking foods have changed. We do it now primarily for pleasure, not for preservation. Basically, though, smoking is still about cooking food at some distance from a smoldering fire that burns with wood.

If that sounds like barbecue to you, you are right, but smoking has always been (and still is) much bigger than barbecue's relatively narrow focus on big cuts of tough meat that require hours and hours of gentle cooking before surrendering to tenderness. I have included in this book several authentic recipes for barbecue classics, such as beef brisket, pulled pork, and a version of spare-ribs that is reminiscent of what I ate 30 years ago in rural Louisiana. As much as I adore barbecue, I wanted to write a book about a much wider spectrum of smoked foods and I wanted to share with you many of the quickly grilled items that are improved with a little smoke. So, for example, I knew that marinated rib eye steaks make a feast for the senses when grilled over charcoal, but why not add some wood chips to the coals and also throw in some woody sprigs of fresh thyme? Let me tell you, the results are tremendous. Unbounded by any presumptions about what can or cannot be smoked, I let my creativity run wild. I think you'll see some examples of that in recipes like Shrimp and Rice Sausages with Vietnamese Dipping Sauce (see page 143) and Cedar-Planked Brie with Cherry Chutney and Toasted Almonds (see page 42). In several cases I have adapted authentic regional recipes; however, each adaptation is based on certain truths I have learned about smoking. These truths have cleared up the mystery for me.

One of these truths is that smoke is a type of seasoning. Great cooks develop a sense about how much of any particular seasoning to use in any given dish. They learn from more experienced cooks and from cookbooks. In this book you will learn that with smoke, less is often more. In fact, the most common mistake among beginners is to use too much smoke, which turns food bitter and sooty. For each recipe in this book, I recommend a certain kind of wood and a certain length of smoking time, so please start with those recommendations. If you like a deeper smoke flavor, add a little more wood next time.

Another truth about smoking is that temperature is paramount. If you can control your fire to remain in a narrow range of heat, and if your grill can burn wood cleanly, you are well on your way to some excellent smoked foods. But if the temperature in your grill rises and falls out of the right range, the food is bound to suffer. The fact that you can smoke food on a water smoker or a charcoal grill is so well-known that I hardly need to mention it here, but I should emphasize that a gas grill is also a viable option for smoking. Why? Because nothing controls temperatures, even the very low temperatures that we often use for smoking, as easily as a gas grill. If the grill is equipped with a metal smoker box, and preferably a dedicated burner right under that smoker box, you have a reliable scenario for excellent smoking. Just set the temperature, start the wood chips burning, and position the food the right distance from the heat. For many more details on smoking on a charcoal grill, a water smoker, or a gas grill, see pages 18 to 23. Everything you'll need to get started is covered there. You will see that each type of grill works differently. For instance, during long cooking sessions, a charcoal grill will require a lot more fire tending than a water smoker, but really, you can smoke food on any grill.

Many of the other truths I've learned are included in the recipes themselves. With each one I've written special tips and instructions to help you focus on the required elements for success. In some cases, I draw your attention to a particular way of cutting meat or brining poultry prior to cooking. In other cases, the "secret" is in how to build the fire, when to add the wood chips, or how to determine doneness. As you try more and more of the recipes, you will find that there really is no great mystery about smoking foods; there are just some simple fundamentals to follow.

As much as I adore barbecue, I wanted to write a book about a much wider spectrum of smoked foods and I wanted to share with you many of the quickly grilled items that are improved with a little smoke.

I think of this book as a course that begins with the basics, helping you get past any confusion or intimidation about the topic, and then teaches you a set of skills and techniques to rely on in almost any smoked recipe. It, of course, also provides you with plenty of options for refining what you've learned. You may start with a simple Cedar-Planked Tuna Salad (see page 154) or Oak-Roasted Leg of Lamb (see page 77), but if you are like many of us who have let a hobby turn into an obsession, it won't be long before you are tackling recipes like Brined and Maple Smoked Bacon (see page 91), Smoked Trout and Artichoke Dip (see page 41), and Peppery Beef Jerky (see page 65). My hope is that you will emerge on the other side of this course with a thorough understanding, a fearless attitude, and a greater hunger to explore the not-so-mysterious world of smoke cooking.

Jamie Purviance

TABLE OF CONTENTS

5

7

6

8

POULTRY SEAFOOD VEGETABLES AND SIDES RESOURCES

Smoking Basics

THE BASICS OF FIRE

At the beginning of man's history with smoking, the only real choice of fuel was wood. Today some backyard cooks still swear by this fuel, even though wood is actually pretty inefficient for cooking or smoking purposes. It often takes more than an hour for the blazing hot flames to settle down to the point where you get a good, consistent heat, and occasionally, freshly cut logs produce a dark smoke that can taint food with a sooty taste. These negatives and others have led to some excellent alternatives.

PURE HARDWOOD CHARCOAL. Pure hardwood charcoal, sometimes called "lump charcoal," is made entirely from hardwood logs that have been heated at high temperatures but with very little oxygen so they won't burn. Instead, the moisture, sap, and resins in the wood are volatilized and vaporized, leaving behind only combustible carbon. The logs eventually break down into black lumps of carbonized hardwood that light faster than wood logs and maintain a relatively even range of temperatures. As hardwood charcoal burns, it releases clean wisps of aromatic smoke reflecting the type of wood used to make the charcoal. However, not all lump charcoal is the same. Look for a kind of wood you like (for example, mesquite, oak, or a combination) and choose bags filled with big lumps, about the size of your fist, that clearly show real wood grain. Some brands will try to sell you "hardwood charcoal" made from scraps of wood flooring or other building construction bits and pieces. These are not nearly as good.

BENEFIT: *Lights quickly and produces aromatic smoke that reflects the variety of wood used to make it.*

HARDWOOD BRIQUETTES. The compressed black pillows of hardwood briquettes are made from crushed pieces of hardwood charcoal. You wouldn't want to buy crushed pieces alone because they would burn out too quickly, but in hardwood briquettes those pieces are held together with a natural starch, usually cornstarch. Plus, hardwood briquettes are so densely packed that they actually burn longer and more evenly than oddly shaped lumps of hardwood charcoal that have more surface area exposed to oxygen. One reason why the briquettes are generally more popular than the lump charcoal for smoking is that they burn at predictably even temperatures. The briquettes don't create as much aromatic smoke, but it is easy enough to add wood chips or chunks to get all the smoke you want.

BENEFIT: *Achieves a longer, more consistent burn than pure hardwood charcoal, but with less woodsy smoke.*

STANDARD CHARCOAL BRIQUETTES. The most commonly available briquettes are compressed bundles of ground charcoal, coal, and other materials, such as clay and limestone, along with binders like cornstarch. While they don't produce quite as much heat as pure hardwood charcoal or hardwood briquettes, smoking rarely requires high heat, and these briquettes do very well at holding steady temperatures in either a charcoal grill or a smoker. In fact, they often burn longer than hardwood briquettes. When you add wood chips or chunks to standard smoldering briquettes, you have everything you need for a first-class smoking scenario. Just one caution: briquettes that have been made with lighter fluid to help them catch fire faster can flavor your food with an oily, sooty taste. Stick with regular briquettes and light them with a chimney starter (see page 10 for more on this).

BENEFIT: *Burns longer than pure hardwood briquettes and holds steady temperatures in both charcoal grills and smokers.*

GAS. Compared to any kind of wood or charcoal, gas has at least one advantage: it burns cleanly at the precise temperature(s) you want. As long as there's enough gas in the tank, a good gas grill will burn at almost any temperature, including the very low temperatures preferred for most smoking recipes. The smoky flavor achieved with a gas grill alone is not at all the same as what you get with wood smoke. It is the result of fats and juices dripping onto the angled metal bars that protect the burners. They vaporize and turn into their own appealing smoke. Nevertheless, a gas grill equipped with a smoker box that is filled with wood chips can easily pump out glorious clouds of wood smoke (see page 22 for more on this).

BENEFIT: *Provides the most precise temperatures and the cleanest burn.*

LIGHTING CHARCOAL

First and foremost, please light your charcoal in a completely safe and reliable way. The best method is to use a chimney starter, which is a metal cylinder with a handle on the outside and a wire rack on the inside.

1] Begin soaking wood chips in water (it's not necessary to soak wood chunks). A disposable foil pan works well for this. Make sure the chips are almost entirely submerged in the water for at least 30 minutes.

2] Remove the cooking grate from your grill and place the chimney starter on the charcoal grate below. Fill the space under the wire rack with a couple sheets of wadded-up newspaper, and fill the space above the rack with charcoal. (As an alternative, use paraffin cubes in place of newspaper.) Because most smoked recipes call for low to medium heat, you won't always need to fill the chimney completely with charcoal. Sometimes it's best to start smoking recipes with just enough charcoal to fill one-third to one-half of the chimney. Avoid using lighter fluid—you don't need it.

3] Light the newspaper through the holes on the side of the chimney. The beauty of this method is that the chimney pushes air up through the coals, lighting them much faster and more evenly than if the coals are spread out.

If you don't have a chimney starter, you can also build a pyramid of charcoal briquettes over a few paraffin cubes, and light the cubes.

Now wait (but never leave a grill unattended). With adequate ventilation, lump charcoal will be fully lit in 15 to 20 minutes, briquettes in 25 to 35 minutes. Briquettes will develop a light coating of white ash when fully lit; lump charcoal will show white ash just around the edges. If you wait too long, either type of charcoal will disintegrate into powder.

DIRECT VERSUS INDIRECT HEAT

Having enough heat is one thing, but what really matters is what you do with that heat.

The first and most fundamental choice you face is whether to use direct heat or indirect heat.

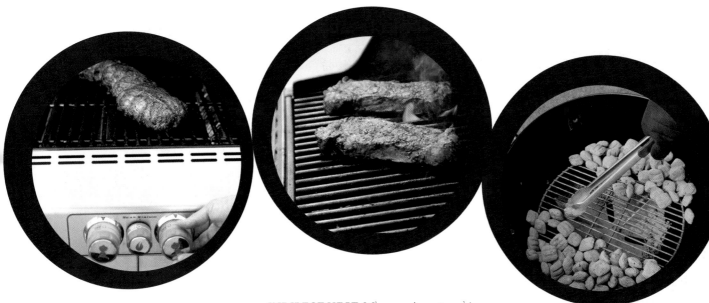

DIRECT HEAT. Direct heat is the heat right under your food. If your food is cooking directly over hot charcoal or directly over the lit burners of a gas grill, you are cooking with direct heat. This strong, radiant heat is the kind most people associate with grilling, though it sometimes creates fantastic, caramelized flavors and textures even when smoking.

Direct heat works great for small, tender pieces of food that cook quickly, such as hamburgers, steaks, chops, boneless chicken pieces, fish fillets, shellfish, and sliced vegetables. It sears the surface of these foods, developing flavors, textures, and caramelization while it cooks the food all the way to the center.

INDIRECT HEAT. When you're not cooking food directly over the heat, or if the food is somehow shielded from direct heat, you are using indirect heat. For example, if the coals are burning on one side of the grill and your food is smoking on the opposite side, you are using indirect heat. If the burners on the left and right sides of your gas grill are lit, but the burners in the middle are unlit and the food is smoking in the middle, you are cooking with indirect heat.

Indirect heat works better for larger, tougher foods that require longer cooking times, such as roasts, whole chickens, and ribs. It is also the proper way to finish cooking thicker foods or bone-in cuts that have been seared or browned first over direct heat.

SOME OF EACH HEAT. There are times when it's wise to cook with both direct and indirect heat—even when smoking. For example, you may want to start cooking bone-in chicken thighs over direct heat to sear and brown the outsides, and then move them over indirect heat to finish. If you try to cook the thighs over direct heat only, you will probably burn the outsides before the meat in the center is fully cooked.

The combination of two heats allows for both beautifully browned outsides and thoroughly cooked interiors. If you want to smoke those thighs, simply add wood chips to the charcoal or to the gas grill's smoker box after you move the thighs over indirect heat.

THE BASIC EQUIPMENT

According to most food historians, the first "smokers" were nothing more than racks of tree branches suspended high over smoldering embers to smoke and preserve whole fish and slabs of meat. Eventually cooks realized that covering the food and the fire gave them a lot more control over the temperatures and the smoke. Now backyard cooks have several good options for covered smokers. Let's open the lid on some of the most popular.

CHARCOAL GRILL. This one is most often associated with grilling, but grilling and smoking are in fact very close cousins in the family of outdoor cooking. Since so many people already have a charcoal grill, they usually start their smoking adventures here. The typical approach is to create a small charcoal fire on one side of the charcoal grate, and then position the food on the opposite side of the grill (on the cooking grate). When you add wood to the charcoal and close the lid, you are smoking in every sense of the word. But that's just the beginning. Then you need to control the heat by minding the coals and adjusting the vents for the right amount of airflow. It's a live fire, and you are actively participating in how it burns.

WATER SMOKER. Many outdoor cooks take great pleasure in minding the coals of a charcoal grill, but smoking often requires very low temperatures, and tending a small bed of coals in a charcoal grill can be quite challenging. A water smoker eliminates the need to be as actively involved in the fire. This smoker can hold temperatures from 200° to 250°F for at least four hours, often longer, depending on the type of fuel. The Weber version is an upright, bullet-shaped unit with three sections. The charcoal and wood burn in the bottom section, which is designed with vents for controlling airflow. The water pan in the middle section acts as a shield between the charcoal and the food, which means the heat is indirect. The food sits on one or two racks above the water pan, and the top section is a domed lid, which has a thermometer and an adjustable vent.

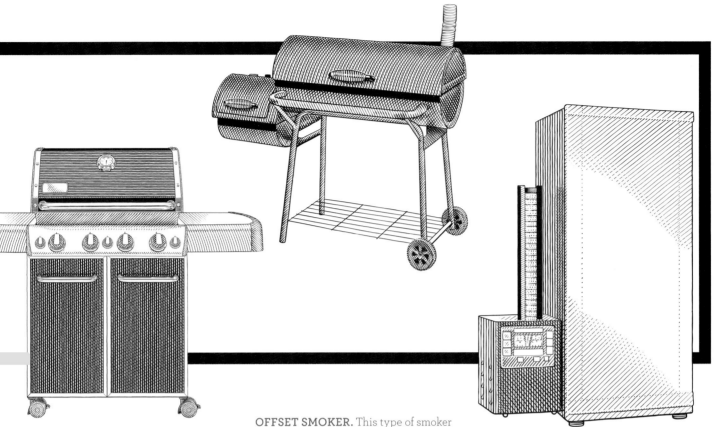

GAS GRILL. You may be a bit surprised to learn that gas grills can do an excellent job of smoking foods. Actually most large-scale, commercial smoking done around the world today for favorites like smoked fish and sausages is achieved with gas smokers, because it's much easier to maintain ideal smoking temperatures. What's true for commercial smokers is also true for backyard gas grills: if you set the gas grill for the ideal temperature and burn wood chips in the grill's metal smoker box, you can smoke almost any food with top-quality results. In most cases, you will light some but not all of the burners, and then smoke the food on an area of the cooking grate not directly over a lit burner. By adjusting the temperature of the burner under the smoker box, you can control how quickly or slowly the chips release their fragrant smoke.

OFFSET SMOKER. This type of smoker is called "offset" because the charcoal and wood burn inside a box (the "firebox") that is off to the side of the main cooking chamber. This particular design prevents the cooking chamber from getting too hot. There is a baffle (or vent) on the outside of the firebox to help you control how much air is getting to the charcoal, and a baffle on top of the chimney extending above the cooking chamber so you can accelerate or decelerate how quickly air and smoke pass through the smoker. This design has evolved from basic barrel smokers of yesteryear: empty oil barrels cut in half, fitted with a cooking grate, and laid on their sides so embers and wood could burn at one end of the barrel and food could smoke at the other.

REFRIGERATOR-STYLE SMOKER. This smoker is for folks who want to smoke more than 25 pounds of food at once. The design is similar in some respects to that of an off-set smoker; that is, the firebox is situated to the side of the cooking chamber. Originally these smokers were made from old refrigerators, because they were cheap and the walls were well insulated. But the concept worked so well that some manufacturers have adapted the design to include digital technology that allows you to program the temperature, the smoking time, and even the amount of smoke, often generated by little wood pellets that are slowly fed into an electric firebox for a hands-off smoking experience.

MUST-HAVE TOOLS

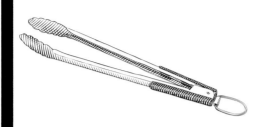

CHIMNEY STARTER

The simple design lets you start charcoal quickly and evenly without using lighter fluid. Look for one with two handles—one side handle for lifting and a hinged top handle for support—and a capacity to hold at least five quarts of briquettes (80 to 100 pieces).

TONGS

Without a doubt, the most useful tool of all. Have at least three pairs: one for raw food, one for cooked food, and one for handling charcoal and wood. Look for heavy-duty tongs that are about 16 inches long, feel comfortable in your hand, have sturdy metal pincers, and are dishwasher safe. A locking mechanism is nice for keeping them closed when not in use.

GRILL BRUSH

Spring for a sturdy, long-handled brush with stiff stainless steel bristles.

INSTANT-READ THERMOMETER

If you want to smoke meat like a pro, this is the surest way to check for doneness. You can buy an inexpensive thermometer with a dial face or a more expensive one with a digital face. Ideally the sensor will be very close to the tip so you can easily pinpoint the area of the food you want to measure.

DISPOSABLE FOIL PANS

Have these on hand for soaking wood chips, creating a water pan, or just moving food to and from your grill. You can cook with them, too, capturing precious juices.

INSULATED BARBECUE MITTS

Invest in a pair with good-quality materials and workmanship that will hold up well over time.

RIB RACK

This clever item saves space on your grill by standing racks of ribs upright rather than laying them flat. Now you can smoke four racks of ribs where previously you could only smoke two.

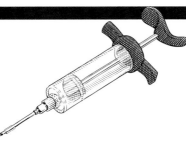

INJECTOR

One of the trade secrets of many barbecue champions is enhancing the meat prior to smoking with a savory brine or marinade. This is the tool for distributing that liquid evenly inside the meat.

SPICE SHAKER

Keep a batch of your magic seasonings in one of these shakers so that you can quickly and evenly distribute the spices with a few flicks of the wrist.

STEEL BUCKET

Smart outdoor cooks pour their hot charcoal ashes into one of these before throwing them away. A steel bucket is also a safe place for a chimney starter filled with lit charcoal. Place only on a noncombustible surface.

SPRAY BOTTLE

Fill one with apple juice and vinegar for keeping smoked meats moist.

TIMER

If timing is everything, then having a good timer makes all the difference. The best ones have extra large digits for easy reading, loud alarms, and the flexibility to count up from zero as well as down from whatever time you pick.

THE SMOKE

You could power a hot air balloon around the world with all the opinions about which types of wood smoke go best with certain kinds of food.

The truth is, there is no absolute right answer. We're talking about a matter of personal taste. So if you prefer a particular type of wood with a particular kind of food, well then, that's your right answer. If you aren't sure about your favorite wood-and-food combinations, start with the suggestions on the next page and feel free to agree or disagree however you like. That's part of the sport we call barbecue.

At most stores you will find smoking wood sold either in chips or chunks. Each calls for a slightly different way of handling.

CHIPS. These little slivers of wood have been "chipped" roughly to expose a lot of surface area and should almost always be soaked in water for at least 30 minutes. Otherwise, they are likely to catch fire and raise the temperature of the grill. They are easy to add to a bed of burning charcoal or to a gas grill's smoker box, and a couple handfuls will provide 10 to 20 minutes of smoke, depending on how hot the fire is. The one time when you don't soak chips is when you want to add them to charcoal for a short burst of flames and heat.

CHUNKS. These range from golf ball–sized to pieces as big as softballs. The usual size is about as big as a fist and will smolder for a couple of hours on a bed of charcoal, though it is too big for a gas grill's smoker box. Water doesn't manage to seep into chunks any deeper than about ¼ inch, so there is not much sense in spending half an hour or so just to get the wood's outer surface wet. If you are concerned about them catching fire (which rarely happens), arrange the chunks along the outer edge of the bed of charcoal.

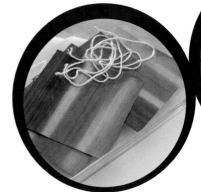

PAPERS. A relatively new entry onto the smoking stage, these thin pieces of wood (usually cedar) should be submerged in water for at least 10 minutes before being wrapped around whatever you want to smoke. Tie the bundles with butcher's twine, and then grill them on all sides to produce light amounts of sweet smoke.

PLANKS. Flat and skinny, these boards come in several sizes, from squares barely as big as a pork chop to rectangles long enough to hold an entire side of salmon. All planks should be submerged in water and soaked for at least one hour before being charred on a grill. Once a plank is charred on one side and it begins to smolder, flip it over, arrange the food on top, and let it smoke for as long as the recipe suggests.

WHAT GOES WITH WHAT?

Most cooks agree that wood smoke comes in varying strengths or intensities, from mild to moderate to strong. It's a good idea to match the intensity of the smoke to the intensity of your food. The chart at the right provides some suggestions.

Also know that you don't have to confine yourself to just one type of wood. Sometimes you can achieve the most wonderful results by mixing two or three kinds of wood together. For example, a 50/50 mix of hickory and apple produces a sweet-smelling smoke that is also hearty enough for barbecued ribs or brisket. If you want to get even more creative, consider adding one of these other options to your grill:

Grapevines
Herb stems
Lavender branches
Rosemary branches
Soaked black peppercorns
Soaked cardamom pods
Soaked cinnamon sticks
Tea leaves

CAUTION. It may be tempting to throw any kind of wood onto the fire, including the wood from a fallen tree in your backyard, but be warned. Some wood, particularly softwoods like pine and aspen, can create bitter smoke that may in fact be toxic. And make sure any wood, herbs, or vines you use have not been treated with harmful chemicals or "finished" in some way. If it's in the smoke, it's on your food.

WOOD TYPE	CHARACTERISTICS	PAIR WITH
Alder	**MILD:** Delicate flavor that is particularly nice with fish	Salmon, swordfish, sturgeon, other fish, poultry, pork
Apple	**MILD:** Slightly sweet but also dense, fruity smoke flavor	Beef, poultry, game birds, pork (particularly ham)
Cherry	**MILD:** Slightly sweet, fruity smoke flavor	Poultry, game birds, pork
Peach or pear	**MILD:** Slightly sweet, woodsy flavor	Poultry, game birds, pork
Hickory	**MODERATE:** Pungent, smoky, bacon-like flavor	Pork, poultry, beef, wild game, cheeses
Maple	**MODERATE:** Mildly smoky, somewhat sweet flavor	Poultry, vegetables, ham
Oak	**MODERATE:** An assertive but pleasing flavor; sometimes a little acidic; blends well with sweeter woods	Beef (particularly brisket), poultry, pork
Pecan	**MODERATE:** Rich and more subtle than hickory, but similar in taste; burns cool, so ideal for very low heat smoking	Pork, poultry, lamb, fish, cheeses
Mesquite	**STRONG:** In a class by itself—a big, bold smoke bordering on bitter	Beef and lamb

HOW TO SMOKE ON A CHARCOAL GRILL

The most useful way to set up your charcoal grill for smoking is to create a two-zone fire. That simply means you arrange the coals on one side of the charcoal grate and leave the other side empty, giving yourself two heat zones. One will have direct heat and the other will have indirect heat.

TO PREPARE THE GRILL, FOLLOW THESE STEPS:

1]

Before you light the charcoal, find out how much wood the recipe suggests and soak wood chips in water for at least 30 minutes so that they will smolder and smoke rather than flame up (no need to soak wood chunks). Light the charcoal as shown on page 10. More often than not, you will need only a small bed of charcoal for smoking, so start with the chimney filled about halfway. The swinging handle above the chimney starter is there to help you lift and aim the chimney where you want it. Be sure to wear insulated barbecue mitts when handling the chimney starter.

2]

Pour the lit charcoal on one side of the charcoal grate, either right onto the grate or into a charcoal basket. Put the empty chimney starter on a heatproof surface away from children and pets. If the coals are not in a charcoal basket, use long-handled tongs to arrange them so that they cover one-third to one-half of the charcoal grate. It's okay if the coals are piled one or two coals deep, but no more than that. Remember, you will probably need medium or low indirect heat, so start with a small amount of charcoal and add more later as needed.

3]

For recipes that involve more than 30 minutes of cooking time, place a water pan on the empty side of the charcoal grate. Fill the pan about three-quarters of the way with water. The pan will catch any juices and fat from the food. Plus, the water will absorb and release heat slowly, evening out the temperatures and adding a bit of moisture to the smoking process.

Make sure to sweep away any ashes that have accumulated on the bottom of the bowl, and leave the bottom vents open all the way. Now preheat the grill.

4]

Put the cooking grate in place (if the grate has hinged sides, arrange one of the hinged sides over the charcoal so that it will be easy to add more charcoal later without taking the grate off the grill). Then put the lid on the grill and open the top vent completely. Now wait until the temperature reaches the right range for the recipe you are making (see "How Hot Should the Fire Be" on the facing page). Keep in mind that as the charcoal burns, the temperature will drop. When the temperature reaches the upper end of your desired temperature range, remove the lid and use a long-handled grill brush to scrape off any bits and pieces of food that may be sticking to the cooking grate.

5]

Drain and add the required amount of wood chips evenly over the charcoal. The chips should be damp but not so wet that they could put out the fire. The damp chips will initially drop the temperature of the fire, but the heat will recover once the chips begin to smolder. Put the lid on the grill and wait for smoke to start pouring out of the grill. Open the lid and arrange the food on the cooking grate as the recipe suggests. Close the lid and position it so that the vent is on the side of the grill opposite the charcoal; this will draw the heat and smoke over the food and out the vent.

6]

If you will be cooking for more than 30 minutes, you will probably need to add more charcoal over time. If you are using standard charcoal briquettes, add them when they are fully lit, because the taste of food sometimes suffers when it absorbs the aromas of partially lit briquettes. Fortunately pure hardwood charcoal and hardwood briquettes don't produce any unwanted aromas in the early stages of their burning, so you can add those to the fire when they are unlit or lit.

The grill vents control the airflow. The more air flowing into the grill, the hotter the fire will grow and the more frequently you will have to replenish it. To minimize that, keep the lid closed as much as possible, but the vents on the bottom of the grill should (almost always) be left open whenever you are cooking. To slow the rate of your fire's burn, close the top vent as much as three-quarters of the way.

All kinds of charcoal, especially briquettes made with fillers, will leave some ash after all the combustible carbon has burned. If you allow the ashes to accumulate on the bottom of the grill, they will eventually cover the vents and starve the coals of air, eventually putting them out. So, every hour or so, give the vents a gentle sweep to clear them of ashes.

HOW HOT SHOULD THE FIRE BE?

You will be working with five temperature ranges:

1] High: 450° to 550°F
2] Medium: 350° to 450°F
3] Low: 250° to 350°F
4] Very low: 200° to 225°F
5] Extremely low: about 175°F

A thermometer on the lid of the grill is the most reliable way to check the temperature. If your grill doesn't have one, you can try the "feel the heat" method. Spread out your hand, palm down, five inches above the charcoal grate. If you have to move your hand in 2 to 4 seconds, you have high heat; in 5 to 7 seconds, medium heat; 8 to 10 seconds, low heat; 11 to 12 seconds, very low heat; and 13 to 15 seconds, extremely low heat.

HOW TO SMOKE ON A WATER SMOKER

A water smoker allows you to smoke foods at consistent temperatures below 250°F for several hours—something that is quite challenging to do with a charcoal grill. The design is basically an upright bullet made of three sections. The charcoal burns in the bottom section. The water sits in a pan in the middle section, preventing any fat from dripping onto the coals and, more importantly, keeping the temperature nice and low. Your food sits on one or two racks in the middle section. The top section is the lid, which includes a vent and a thermometer.

TO PREPARE THE SMOKER, FOLLOW THESE STEPS:

1] First of all, remove the top and middle sections from the bottom section. Lay the charcoal grate in the bottom section and set the charcoal ring on top of the grate. Fill a chimney starter to the top with charcoal and pour the charcoal into the ring, spreading it out evenly. Now, if you are using a 22½-inch-diameter smoker, fill the chimney starter with charcoal again and light the charcoal in a completely safe and reliable way, as shown on page 10. If you are using an 18-inch-diameter smoker, fill the chimney starter only halfway with charcoal and light it safely.

2] As soon as the briquettes are lightly covered with gray ash (or once the lump charcoal is lit around all the edges), carefully pour the lit charcoal over the unlit charcoal, spreading it out evenly. Over time the unlit charcoal will burn and extend the life of the fire.

3] Make sure the water pan is empty and suspended inside the middle section and the charcoal access door is closed. Set the middle section over the bottom section.

4] Immediately, before the water pan gets too hot, fill it about three-quarters full with water. Next, set the two cooking grates in place inside the middle section. Now place the lid on top. A water smoker has vents on the bottom section and one on the lid.

5]

At this point open the top vent completely and close the bottom vents halfway. Wait until the smoker reaches its ideal temperature range of 225° to 250°F.

Open the charcoal access door and, using long-handled tongs, add as many dry wood chunks as the recipe suggests. Close the charcoal access door and wait a few minutes for the smoke to stream out of the vent on the lid.

6]

Remove the lid and arrange the food on the cooking grates, starting with the bottom grate. When you're using both grates, remember this: whatever you have on the top grate will drip onto whatever you have on the bottom grate. It might be delicious if a pork shoulder drips onto a prime rib, but not so delicious if a prime rib drips onto a whole salmon fillet.

Put the lid on the smoker. Wait for 10 to 15 minutes to see if the temperature returns to the ideal range (225° to 250°F). Often the food will bring down the temperature inside the smoker. If the temperature is too low, open the bottom vents a bit more. If the temperature is too high, close the top vent as much as halfway, but never close the top vent all the way.

TENDING THE FIRE

A water smoker can maintain temperatures in the range of 225° to 250°F for several hours with no added fuel.

One of the reasons for this is the water pan. Positioned between the fire and the food, the water regulates the smoker's temperature to a certain extent by absorbing or releasing heat. The less air you allow into the smoker, the lower the temperature will go. To raise the temperature, open the bottom vents. You can also add more charcoal through the access door in the middle section, though this is rarely necessary for recipes that cook in less than four hours. The charcoal can be unlit or lit, though standard briquettes are prone to emit an acrid aroma at first, producing a taste that can spoil the fruits of your labor, so either light those briquettes first in a chimney starter, or use lump charcoal or hardwood briquettes to refuel the smoker.

Open the top lid as little as possible while smoking. When no smoke is streaming out of the top vent, you may want to add more wood chunks to the coals below—although not too many or too often. It's easy (and awful) to overdo it. The smoke should flow like a gentle stream, not like it is billowing out of a train engine.

Every couple of hours, refill the water pan to maintain the proper temperature range.

HOW TO SMOKE ON A GAS GRILL

Setting up a gas grill for smoking can be very easy, especially if the grill is equipped with a built-in smoker box; however, there is a way to create smoke even without a built-in smoker box.

First, start soaking wood chips in water (check the recipe for the amount you'll need). They should soak in water for at least 30 minutes or else they are likely to light on fire and give you more flame than smoke.

TO PREPARE THE GRILL, FOLLOW THESE STEPS:

1]

Follow all safety and lighting instructions when lighting a gas grill.

To light a gas grill, first open the lid so unlit gas fumes don't collect in the cooking box.

2]

Now slowly open the valve on your propane tank (or natural gas line) all the way and wait a minute for the gas to travel through the gas line.

3]

Turn on the burners, including the dedicated burner under the smoker box, setting them all to high. Close the lid and preheat the grill for 10 to 15 minutes.

When the temperature reaches 500°F, use a long-handled grill brush to clean the cooking grates. In most cases, you will be smoking with indirect (and usually low) heat. Turn off the burner(s) in the middle and turn down the outside burners to the suggested temperature in the recipe. For now, keep the dedicated burner under the smoker box turned to high.

5] Arrange the food in the middle of the cooking grate, over the unlit burner(s). Close the lid as soon as possible and let the food cook.

Controlling the temperature of a gas grill is not a matter of opening and closing vents, it's simply a matter of turning knobs. In most cases you will adjust one or two of the main burners during cooking, though if you want to smoke at very low temperatures (below 250°F), turn off all of the main burners and use just the dedicated burner under the smoker box for the heat. Keep in mind that most of the smoke will accumulate around the smoker box. The closer your food is to the smoker box, the more smoke flavor it will absorb.

4] Using long-handled tongs, open the lid of the smoker box. Grab some of the soaked wood chips with the tongs, let the excess water drain off, and drop the wood chips into the smoker box. Spread out the wood chips so they cover the bottom of the box, directly exposing as many chips as possible to the burner below. Continue to add as many wood chips as the recipe suggests. Close the lid of the smoker box.

Close the lid of the grill and wait a few minutes for smoke to pour out of the grill. Now it's time to lower the heat of the dedicated burner under the smoker box to medium or low so that the wood will smolder slowly.

IF YOUR GRILL DOESN'T HAVE A BUILT-IN SMOKER BOX

BUY ONE

Nowadays you can purchase a heavy-gauge stainless steel smoker box to sit right on top of your cooking grate. The metal will conduct the heat of your grill to the soaked wood chips you pile inside the box. The holes in the lid will direct the fragrant smoke over your food. When the wood chips have burned out, you can simply open the lid and add more, if you like.

MAKE YOUR OWN

Place drained wood chips in a foil pan, cover with aluminum foil, and poke holes in the foil to allow the smoke to escape. Place the pan directly on the bars over an unlit burner or two, preferably in a back corner. Put the cooking grates in place. Turn on the grill, with all the burners on high, and close the lid. When smoke appears, begin cooking your food, adjusting the temperature of the grill as needed. You can't add more chips to the pan, but at least it's a start.

BRINGING ON EVEN MORE FLAVOR

Whenever you smoke foods, remember that your main ingredient is like the lead singer in a rock-and-roll band. Every other ingredient, including the smoke, should make the main ingredient better.

It would be a shame to smother something inherently wonderful like a well-marbled slab of pork ribs under a blanket of spices and sauce, but even the most fabulous main ingredients can often be improved with a few judicious layers of flavor. By adding one or more of the options outlined below, you have a chance to distinguish your food with an ethnic authenticity or a creative spin that reflects your personal style. This act of layering flavors—and balancing them with the smoke for a harmonic effect—is what separates the masters from the masses.

RUBS. A rub is a mixture of ground spices, herbs, and other seasonings, sometimes including sugar. The term comes from massaging the meat with the seasonings, but you will actually do better to sprinkle the rub over the main ingredient from a distance of six inches or more so that you distribute it evenly without roughing up the surface of the main ingredient. Rubs work best when there's a little salt in the mix, because salt has a way of creating openings in the surface of the food—allowing flavors, including smoke flavors, to penetrate deeper.

MARINADES. Wet marinades tend to work more slowly than rubs, but over time they can seep in even farther, and often their acidic elements like vinegar or citrus juices help to tenderize meats. Marinades typically include a fair amount of oil, too, which can help a lot when a particular meat, fish, or vegetable lacks enough richness on its own to be smoked for a long time. Smoke compounds are fat and water soluble, so the added moisture can also help marinated foods absorb smoke a bit better.

BRINES. These salty solutions are really just intense versions of marinades, but their high concentration of salt means that they work on the main ingredients a little differently. The salt is able to open up pathways in the meat and carry moisture and flavors deep inside. Long periods of smoking tend to dry out meats, so brines are often effective antidotes to this concern.

SAUCES. Barbecue sauces, sticky glazes, savory relishes, slow-cooked chutneys, flavored butters, thin mop sauces, luscious vinaigrettes ... the possibilities go on and on. The world of sauces is so vast that it is hard to know which ones are best for smoked foods and how to make them. The next several pages address those important questions.

A SMOKER'S PANTRY AND SPICE RACK

The basis of great cooking begins with ingredients. What you do with those ingredients may prove to be even more important. Hopefully you will bring time-tested techniques, your own intuition, and a spark of imagination to your cooking, but first let's spell out the critical ingredients that you will use again and again when layering the flavors of smoked food. These are the most useful for making rubs, marinades, brines, and sauces.

OILS
Canola oil
Extra-virgin olive oil
Toasted sesame oil

SWEETENERS
Apple juice
Brown sugar
Granulated sugar
Honey
Maple syrup
Molasses
Soft drinks

TOMATO PRODUCTS
Ketchup
Tomato paste
Tomato sauce

SAUCES AND MUSTARDS
Dijon mustard
Hoisin sauce
Soy sauce
Worcestershire sauce
Yellow mustard

VINEGARS
Balsamic vinegar
Cider vinegar
Red wine vinegar
Rice vinegar
White wine vinegar

OTHER
Beer
Chicken and beef broth
Cocoa powder
Horseradish
Hot pepper sauce
Liquid smoke

DRIED HERBS
Basil
Bay leaves
Dill
Marjoram
Oregano
Parsley
Rosemary
Sage
Tarragon
Thyme

SPICES
Allspice
Black pepper
Cayenne pepper
Celery seed
Chinese five spice
Cinnamon
Cloves
Coriander
Crushed red pepper flakes
Cumin
Curry powder
Fennel seed
Ginger
Granulated garlic
Granulated onion
Kosher salt
Mustard powder
Mustard seed
Nutmeg
Paprika
Prepared chili powder
Pure chile powder
Sea salt
Sesame seeds
Turmeric
White pepper

MAKING RUBS

HOT
black pepper
cayenne pepper
crushed red pepper flakes
prepared chili powder
pure chile powder

SWEET
allspice   cloves
brown sugar   granulated sugar
Chinese five spice nutmeg
cinnamon

EARTHY
caraway seed
celery seed
coriander
cumin
paprika

HERBACEOUS (dried herbs)
basil   oregano
bay leaves   parsley
dill   rosemary
fennel   sage
marjoram   thyme

SHARP
granulated garlic
granulated onion
mustard powder
mustard seed
turmeric

SALTY
fleur de sel
kosher salt
sea salt
smoked sea salt

The most interesting spice rubs have a well-orchestrated complexity. There may be several ingredients involved but no single flavor dominates the rest. With that goal in mind, when you make spice rubs for yourself, begin by choosing spices from more than a couple of the six categories pictured here, and keep in mind that each category balances with the one beside it. So, for example, hot spices such as pure chile powder and cayenne pepper have an affinity for sweet elements like brown sugar and cinnamon. Similarly, earthy spices and dried herbs complement each other. The herbs tend to brighten and lighten the deep flavors of spices like cumin and paprika. And if you are using sharp spices like granulated garlic and granulated onion, try adding a bit more salt to mellow out their bite.

MOLE RUB
◊ ◊ ◊
MAKES: about ¼ cup

- 2 tablespoons pure chile powder
- 2 teaspoons unsweetened cocoa powder
- 2 teaspoons packed dark brown sugar
- 1 teaspoon kosher salt
- 1 teaspoon ground black pepper

1 In a small bowl mix the ingredients.

FRENCH ROAST SPICE RUB
◊
MAKES: about 3½ tablespoons

- 2 tablespoons coarsely ground French roast coffee beans
- 2 teaspoons kosher salt
- 1 teaspoon packed light brown sugar
- ¾ teaspoon ground black pepper
- ½ teaspoon granulated garlic

1 In a small bowl mix the ingredients.

RUBS

HOW LONG?

If you leave a rub on for a long time, the seasonings intermix with the juices in the meat and produce more pronounced flavors as well as a crust. This is good to a point, but a rub with a lot of salt or sugar will draw moisture out of the meat over time, making the meat tastier, yes, but also drier. So how long should you use a rub? Here are some guidelines.

TIME	TYPES OF FOOD
Up to 15 minutes	Small foods, such as shellfish, cubed meat for kabobs, and vegetables
15 to 30 minutes	Thin cuts of boneless meat, such as chicken breasts, fish fillets, pork tenderloin, chops, and steaks
30 minutes to 1½ hours	Thicker cuts of boneless or bone-in meat, such as leg of lamb, whole chickens, and beef roasts
2 to 8 hours	Big or tough cuts of meat, such as racks of ribs, whole hams, pork shoulders, and turkeys

LEMON PEPPER SALT

MAKES: about 2 tablespoons
SPECIAL EQUIPMENT: spice mill

- 2   lemons
- 4   teaspoons kosher salt
- 2   teaspoons ground black pepper

1 Preheat the oven to 200°F.

2 Using a vegetable peeler, cut strips of zest from the lemons, avoiding the white, bitter pith. Place the lemon zest on a baking sheet and bake until dry and golden, 30 to 45 minutes. Allow to cool.

3 In a spice mill pulverize the lemon zest. Transfer to a small bowl and mix with the salt and pepper. Use immediately or store in a tightly covered jar for up to 4 weeks.

ANCHO CHILE RUB

MAKES: about ⅔ cup

- 3   tablespoons kosher salt
- 2   tablespoons ancho chile powder
- 2   tablespoons packed light brown sugar
- 2   tablespoons granulated garlic
- 1   tablespoon ground cumin
- 2   teaspoons ground black pepper

1 In a small bowl mix the ingredients.

STEAK HOUSE RUB

MAKES: about 3 tablespoons
SPECIAL EQUIPMENT: spice mill

- 2   teaspoons black peppercorns
- 2   teaspoons mustard seed
- 2   teaspoons paprika
- 1   teaspoon granulated garlic
- 1   teaspoon kosher salt
- 1   teaspoon packed light brown sugar
- ¼   teaspoon pure chile powder

1 In a spice mill crush the peppercorns and mustard seed. Pour into a small bowl and add the remaining ingredients.

SWEET HEAT RUB

MAKES: ⅓ cup

- 2   tablespoons packed dark brown sugar
- 2   teaspoons ground cinnamon
- 2   teaspoons dried thyme
- 2   teaspoons kosher salt
- 2   teaspoons ground black pepper
- 1   teaspoon grated nutmeg
- ½   teaspoon ground allspice
- ½   teaspoon ground mace

1 In a small bowl mix the ingredients.

CHINESE FIVE SPICE RUB

MAKES: 2 tablespoons

- 2   teaspoons granulated garlic
- 1   teaspoon Chinese five spice
- 1   teaspoon ground black pepper
- 1   teaspoon ground coriander
- 1   teaspoon kosher salt

1 In a small bowl mix the ingredients.

PROVENCE RUB

MAKES: 4 teaspoons

- 2   teaspoons herbes de Provence
- 1   teaspoon celery seed
- ½   teaspoon kosher salt
- ¼   teaspoon granulated onion
- ¼   teaspoon ground black pepper

1 In a small bowl mix the ingredients.

KEY
- 🔥 RED MEAT
- 🔥 PORK
- 🔥 POULTRY
- 🔥 SEAFOOD
- 🔥 VEGETABLES

MAKING MARINADES

ACIDS
citrus juices
tomatoes
vinegars
wine
yogurt

OILS
canola oil
extra-virgin olive oil
toasted sesame oil

GOOD FLAVORS
condiments
finely chopped vegetables
fresh or dried herbs
spices
zest of citrus fruits

In marinades you can add whatever you think might taste good, but before you start dumping ingredients into a bowl with all the restraint of a sailor on leave, let me give you some advice. Start with the basics. That means a little acidity, a good deal of oil, and a bunch of other good flavors. The ratio in a basic salad dressing is a good beginning. That's 1:3, or one part acidity to three parts oil. Then add your other flavors. The acidity will tenderize the food, especially the surface of the food, and the oil will provide moisture and richness, as well as carry other flavors. The other flavors, well, they just taste good.

If your marinade includes some acidic liquid, be sure to use a nonreactive container. This is a dish or bowl made of glass, plastic, stainless steel, or ceramic. A container made of aluminum, or some other metals, will react with acids and add a metallic flavor to food.

TANDOORI MARINADE

MAKES: about 2 cups

1½ cups plain Greek yogurt
 1 small yellow onion, chopped
 2 tablespoons chopped fresh ginger
 2 tablespoons fresh lemon juice
 2 tablespoons curry powder
 2 tablespoons paprika
 4 garlic cloves, roughly chopped
 2 teaspoons kosher salt
 ¼ teaspoon ground cayenne pepper

1 In a food processor combine all of the ingredients and process until smooth.

WORCESTERSHIRE PASTE

MAKES: about ⅓ cup

 2 tablespoons extra-virgin olive oil
 2 tablespoons Worcestershire sauce
 2 teaspoons cracked black pepper
 2 teaspoons granulated garlic
1½ teaspoons kosher salt
 1 teaspoon smoked paprika
 1 teaspoon ground cumin
 ½ teaspoon ground cinnamon

1 In a small bowl whisk all of the ingredients.

LEMON MARINADE

MAKES: about ½ cup

 ¼ cup extra-virgin olive oil
 1 tablespoon grated lemon zest
 3 tablespoons fresh lemon juice
 1 tablespoon minced garlic
 1 teaspoon kosher salt
 ½ teaspoon dried thyme

1 In a small bowl whisk all of the ingredients.

TARRAGON-CITRUS MARINADE

MAKES: about 1 cup

 ¼ cup extra-virgin olive oil
 ¼ cup roughly chopped fresh
   tarragon leaves
   Zest and juice of 1 orange
   Zest and juice of 1 lemon
 2 tablespoons sherry vinegar
 2 teaspoons kosher salt
 1 teaspoon minced garlic
 1 teaspoon grated fresh ginger
 ½ teaspoon prepared chili powder
 ½ teaspoon ground black pepper

1 In a small bowl whisk all of the ingredients.

MARINADES

HOW LONG?

The right length of time varies, depending on the strength of the marinade and the food you are marinating. If your marinade includes intense ingredients like soy sauce, hard liquor, or hot chiles and strong spices, don't overdo it. A fish fillet should still taste like fish, not like a burning-hot, salt-soaked piece of protein. Also, if an acidic marinade is left too long on meat or fish, it can turn the surface dry or mushy. Here are some guidelines to get you going.

TIME	TYPES OF FOOD
15 to 30 minutes	Small foods, such as shellfish, fish fillets, cubed meat for kabobs, and tender vegetables
1 to 3 hours	Thin cuts of boneless meat, such as chicken breasts, pork tenderloin, chops, and steaks, as well as sturdy vegetables
2 to 6 hours	Thicker cuts of boneless or bone-in meat, such as leg of lamb, whole chickens, and beef roasts
6 to 12 hours	Big or tough cuts of meat, such as racks of ribs, whole hams, pork shoulders, and turkeys

SOUTHWEST MARINADE

MAKES: about 1 cup

- ½ cup fresh orange juice
- 3 tablespoons extra-virgin olive oil
- 2 tablespoons red wine vinegar
- 1 tablespoon minced garlic
- 2 teaspoons pure chile powder
- 1½ teaspoons dried oregano
- 1 teaspoon kosher salt
- ½ teaspoon ground black pepper
- ½ teaspoon ground cinnamon

1 In a small bowl whisk all of the ingredients.

CREOLE MUSTARD MARINADE

MAKES: about ⅔ cup

- 3 tablespoons Creole mustard
- 3 tablespoons extra-virgin olive oil
- 3 tablespoons red wine vinegar
- 2 teaspoons Worcestershire sauce
- 2 teaspoons minced garlic
- 1 teaspoon dried thyme
- ½ teaspoon kosher salt
- ½ teaspoon ground black pepper

1 In a small bowl whisk all of the ingredients.

TERIYAKI MARINADE

MAKES: about 1¼ cups

- ½ cup pineapple juice
- ½ cup soy sauce
- ¼ cup packed light brown sugar
- 2 tablespoons thinly sliced dark green scallion tops
- 1 tablespoon grated fresh ginger
- 2 teaspoons minced garlic

1 In a medium bowl whisk all of the ingredients until the sugar dissolves.

SWEET BOURBON MARINADE

MAKES: about 2 cups

- ½ cup bourbon
- ½ cup packed light brown sugar
- ⅓ cup soy sauce
- ⅓ cup fresh lemon juice
- 2 tablespoons Worcestershire sauce
- 2 teaspoons finely chopped garlic
- 2 teaspoons finely chopped fresh thyme leaves

1 In a medium bowl whisk all of the ingredients.

POMEGRANATE MARINADE

MAKES: about 1½ cups

- 3 tablespoons pomegranate molasses
- 3 tablespoons balsamic vinegar
- 2 teaspoons finely chopped fresh thyme leaves
- ¾ teaspoon kosher salt
- ½ teaspoon crushed red pepper flakes
- 1 cup extra-virgin olive oil

1 In a medium bowl whisk the molasses, vinegar, thyme, salt, and red pepper flakes. Gradually whisk in the oil.

KEY
- RED MEAT
- PORK
- POULTRY
- SEAFOOD
- VEGETABLES

MAKING BRINES

STEP 1
A well-balanced brine begins with ½ to 1 cup of kosher salt for each gallon of water or other liquid.

STEP 2
Whisk vigorously to dissolve the salt in cold water, and include any herbs and spices you like.

STEP 3
Submerge all areas of the meat in the brine, cover the bowl with plastic wrap, and refrigerate.

When it comes to making brines, the key is to use the right ratio of salt to water. Too much or too little salt can lead to major disappointments. Begin with ½ to 1 cup of kosher salt for each gallon of water or other liquid. This level of saltiness creates a subtle background of flavor inside the meat. What happens is that the salt penetrates the meat and changes the structure of the protein so that the cells inside the meat are able to trap more moisture and flavor. Nature likes equilibrium, so the saltiness inside the meat rises until it is equal to the saltiness in the brine outside the meat. If you like, you can also add sugar to your brine, about the same amount as the salt, and the sugar will complement the saltiness and also caramelize nicely on the surface of the food. Then you can add whatever other flavors you like, including a variety of herbs and spices.

If your brine includes some acidic liquid, be sure to use a nonreactive container. This is a dish or bowl made of glass, plastic, stainless steel, or ceramic. A container made of aluminum, or some other metals, will react with acids and add a metallic flavor to food.

The most deserving candidates for brining are big, lean cuts of meat, such as pork loins and whole turkeys, which you should soak for several hours. But even small items like pork chops, chicken pieces, and salmon fillets are bound to be juicier and more flavorful if you brine them for an hour or two.

Don't be deterred by the thought of always having to spend a long time boiling and cooling a brine, as many cookbooks suggest for dissolving the salt. Just use a light and flaky kosher salt. All you need is a whisk to dissolve that type of salt in cold water.

Whatever you brine should be completely submerged, covered with plastic wrap, and then refrigerated.

ROSEMARY BRINE

MAKES: about 1 gallon

 1 gallon water
 ¾ cup kosher salt
 ½ cup granulated sugar
 2 tablespoons dried rosemary
 1 tablespoon caraway seed
 1 tablespoon granulated garlic
 2 teaspoons ground black pepper

1 In a large pot combine all of the ingredients. Whisk to dissolve the sugar and salt.

BUTTERMILK BRINE

MAKES: about 3 cups

 2 cups cold buttermilk
 1 cup water
 ½ cup kosher salt
 1 tablespoon whole-grain mustard
 1 tablespoon finely chopped fresh tarragon leaves

1 In a medium bowl whisk all of the ingredients until the salt dissolves.

BEER BRINE

MAKES: 2 quarts

 3 bottles (each 12 fluid ounces) lager
3½ cups water
 ½ cup kosher salt
 ½ cup packed light brown sugar

1 In a large pot combine all of the ingredients. Whisk to dissolve the sugar and salt.

BRINES

HARD CIDER BRINE
🔥 🔥

MAKES: about 2 cups

1½ cups hard apple cider
½ cup kosher salt
1 tablespoon dried rosemary
1 tablespoon dried sage
1½ teaspoons dried thyme
½ teaspoon black peppercorns

1 In a medium bowl whisk all of the ingredients until the salt dissolves.

BOURBON BRINE
🔥 🔥

MAKES: about 2 cups

½ cup bourbon
½ cup water
¼ cup packed light brown sugar
2 tablespoons kosher salt
½ teaspoon crushed red pepper flakes
1 cup ice cubes

1 In a medium saucepan over medium heat, combine the bourbon, water, brown sugar, salt, and red pepper flakes. Stir until the sugar and salt dissolve. Remove from the heat and stir in the ice cubes to cool the brine quickly.

CHIPOTLE BRINE
🔥 🔥

MAKES: about 1 quart

1 quart cold water
¼ cup kosher salt
2 tablespoons granulated sugar
1½ teaspoons chipotle chile powder
Zest of 1 lime

1 In a large bowl whisk all of the ingredients until the salt and sugar dissolve.

APPLE BRINE
🔥 🔥

MAKES: about 2¼ quarts

2 quarts chilled unsweetened apple juice, divided
½ cup kosher salt
½ cup soy sauce
3 ounces fresh ginger, thinly sliced
1 tablespoon dried rosemary
1 teaspoon black peppercorns
Zest of 2 lemons, removed in wide strips with a vegetable peeler
2 bay leaves

1 In a medium saucepan over medium heat, combine 1 quart of the apple juice, the salt, soy sauce, ginger, rosemary, peppercorns, lemon zest strips, and bay leaves and bring to a simmer to release the flavors, stirring occasionally. Pour into a large heatproof bowl set in a larger bowl of iced water. Let stand until chilled, about 30 minutes, stirring often. Stir the remaining chilled apple juice into the brine.

SPICY GARLIC BRINE
🔥 🔥 🔥

MAKES: about 6 cups

6 cups cold water
⅓ cup kosher salt
¼ cup granulated sugar
2 medium garlic cloves, peeled and crushed
4 whole allspice, crushed
4 whole cloves, crushed
1 bay leaf, broken in half
1 teaspoon dried marjoram

1 In a large bowl combine the water, salt, and sugar. Whisk until the salt and sugar dissolve. Add the remaining ingredients.

HONEY AND HERB BRINE
🔥 🔥

MAKES: about 2 quarts

2 quarts water
½ cup kosher salt
½ cup honey
2 teaspoons dried rosemary
2 teaspoons dried sage
1½ teaspoons dried marjoram
1 teaspoon black peppercorns
2 bay leaves

1 In a large pot whisk all of the ingredients until the salt dissolves.

CRANBERRY-ORANGE BRINE
🔥 🔥 🔥

MAKES: about 5 quarts

2 quarts cranberry juice
2 quarts fresh orange juice
2 small garlic heads, cloves crushed but not peeled
1 cup kosher salt
¼ cup crushed red pepper flakes
¼ cup fennel seed
4 ounces fresh ginger, thinly sliced
6 bay leaves
4 cups ice cubes

1 In a large, nonreactive pot over high heat, combine all the ingredients, except the ice, and bring to a boil. Boil for about 1 minute and then remove from the heat. Add the ice cubes and allow to cool to room temperature, about 1½ hours.

KEY
🔥 RED MEAT
🔥 PORK
🔥 POULTRY
🔥 SEAFOOD

MAKING SAUCES

SWEET
brown sugar
granulated sugar
hoisin sauce
honey
ketchup
maple syrup
molasses
soft drinks

SOUR
balsamic vinegar
cider vinegar
fresh lemon or lime juice
juice from a pickle or relish jar
mustard
red or white wine vinegar
rice vinegar

SPICY
black pepper
cayenne pepper
crushed red pepper flakes
fresh or dried chiles
horseradish
hot pepper sauces

SALTY
anchovies
fish sauce
kosher salt or sea salt
olives
soy sauce
Worcestershire sauce

If you had to pick just one way to give your food a special edge that reflects your taste, think sauces, but proceed with caution. Sauces represent a giant playground of creativity and, as with marinades, there are almost limitless possibilities, so it's easy to go a little crazy. I suggest starting with a basic barbecue sauce and aiming for a nice blend of sweetness, sourness, spiciness, and saltiness. One way to do this is to choose one or two ingredients from each category on this page. The most traditional barbecue sauces are based on tomato ketchup, for sweetness and thickness, and some version of vinegar, for sourness. After that you can add whatever sources of spiciness and saltiness you prefer. But don't forget that little something extra that really sets a great sauce apart. Let's call it the "extra factor." It could be almost anything. Here are some options to consider.

The "extra" factor:
any spice imaginable
liquid smoke
liquor
wine
tomato sauce
fruit preserves
butter or extra-virgin olive oil
chicken or beef stock
brewed coffee or espresso
you name it ...

SAUCES

RED WINE SAUCE

◊

MAKES: about ¾ cup

1½ cups dry red wine
2 tablespoons minced shallot
1 tablespoon tomato paste
2 teaspoons balsamic vinegar
½ teaspoon Worcestershire sauce
3 tablespoons unsalted butter,
    cut into 3 pieces
    Kosher salt
    Ground black pepper

1 In a small saucepan over high heat, bring the wine and shallot to a boil. Then immediately reduce the heat to medium and simmer until the wine has reduced to about ½ cup, 15 to 20 minutes. Add the tomato paste, vinegar, and Worcestershire sauce. Remove from the heat and add the butter piece by piece, whisking to incorporate the butter into the sauce. Season with salt and pepper.

CREAMY MUSTARD SAUCE

◊ ◊

MAKES: about ¾ cup

1 tablespoon unsalted butter
2 tablespoons minced shallot
½ cup low-sodium beef broth
¾ cup heavy whipping cream
3 tablespoons whole-grain mustard
    Kosher salt

1 In a medium skillet over medium heat, melt the butter. Add the shallot and cook until softened, 1 to 2 minutes, stirring often. Add the broth and bring to a boil over high heat. Cook until the broth reduces by half, 2 to 3 minutes. Add the cream and bring to a simmer (not a boil). Whisk in the mustard and simmer until the sauce is reduced to ¾ cup and is thick enough to coat the back of a spoon, 3 to 5 minutes. Season with salt.

TOMATO-CHIMICHURRI SAUCE

◊ ◊ ◊

MAKES: about 1 cup

1 cup loosely packed fresh Italian
    parsley leaves
½ cup extra-virgin olive oil
⅓ cup loosely packed fresh
    cilantro leaves
¼ cup oil-packed sun-dried
    tomatoes, drained
3 garlic cloves
¾ teaspoon crushed red pepper flakes
    Kosher salt
    Ground black pepper

1 In a food processor combine all the ingredients except the salt and black pepper. Pulse until you get a semi-smooth consistency. Season with salt and pepper.

THREE-HERB HAZELNUT PESTO

◊ ◊ ◊ ◊ ◊

MAKES: about 1¾ cups

½ cup loosely packed fresh
    cilantro leaves
½ cup loosely packed fresh Italian
    parsley leaves
¼ cup loosely packed fresh
    oregano leaves
¼ cup hazelnuts, toasted and
    skins removed
¼ cup sherry vinegar
3–5 medium garlic cloves,
    roughly chopped
½ teaspoon crushed red pepper flakes
½ cup extra-virgin olive oil
    Kosher salt
    Ground black pepper

1 In a food processor, process the fresh herbs, hazelnuts, vinegar, garlic, and red pepper flakes. Then, with the motor running, slowly add the oil to make a thin paste. Season with salt and pepper.

RED CHILE BARBECUE SAUCE

◊ ◊ ◊

MAKES: about 2 cups

4 dried *pasilla* chiles, about ¾ ounce
    total, stems removed
2 tablespoons canola oil
1 cup hot water
½ cup ketchup
3 tablespoons soy sauce
2 tablespoons balsamic vinegar
3 medium garlic cloves, crushed
1 teaspoon ground cumin
½ teaspoon dried oregano
¼ teaspoon kosher salt
¼ teaspoon ground black pepper

1 Cut the chiles crosswise into sections about 2 inches long. Remove most of the seeds. In a medium skillet over high heat, warm the oil. Add the chiles and toast them until they puff up and begin to turn color, 2 to 3 minutes, turning once. Transfer the chiles and oil to a small bowl. Cover with the hot water and soak for 30 minutes. Pour the chiles, along with the oil and water, into a blender or food processor. Add the remaining ingredients and process until very smooth.

KEY
◊ RED MEAT
◊ PORK
◊ POULTRY
◊ SEAFOOD
◊ VEGETABLES

TOP TEN SMOKING TIPS

START EARLY.
Many of the flavor compounds in smoke are fat and water soluble, which means that whatever you are cooking will absorb smoky flavors best when it is raw. As the surface cooks and dries out, the smoke does not penetrate as well.

GO LOW AND SLOW (MOST OF THE TIME).
Real barbecue is cooked slowly over low, indirect heat—with wood smoke—because that's a traditional way to make sinewy meats so moist and tender that you hardly need teeth. But don't miss easy opportunities for adding sweet wood aromas to foods that are grilled over a hot fire for just minutes, like steaks, shrimp, and even vegetables.

REGULATE THE HEAT WITH A WATER PAN.
Big fluctuations in smoking temperatures can tighten and dry out foods. Whenever you cook for longer than an hour with charcoal, use a pan of water to help stabilize the heat and add some humidity. Obviously a water smoker already has one, but for a charcoal grill, use a large disposable foil pan, and don't forget to refill it.

DON'T OVERDO IT.
The biggest mistake rookies make is adding too much wood, chunk after chunk, to the point where the food tastes bitter. In general, you should smoke food for no longer than half its cooking time. Also, the smoke should flow like a gentle stream, not like it is billowing out of a train engine.

WHITE SMOKE IS GOOD; BLACK SMOKE IS BAD.
Clean streams of whitish smoke can layer your food with the intoxicating scents of smoldering wood. But if your fire lacks enough ventilation, or your food is directly over the fire and the juices are burning, blackish smoke can taint your food or lead to unpleasant surprises when you lift the lid.

KEEP THE AIR MOVING.

Keep the vents on your charcoal grill open, and position the vent on the lid on the side opposite the coals. The open vents will draw smoke from the charcoal and wood below so that it swirls over your food and out the top properly, giving you the best ventilation and the cleanest smoke. If the fire gets too hot, close the top vent almost all the way.

DON'T GO GOLFING.

Smoking is a relatively low-maintenance way of cooking—but remain mindful and be safe. Never leave a lit fire unattended, and check the temperature every hour or so. You might need to adjust the vents or add more charcoal.

TRY NOT TO PEEK.

Every time you open a grill, you lose heat and smoke—two of the most important elements for making a great meal. Open the lid only when you really need to tend to the fire, the water pan, or the food. Ideally take care of them all at once—and quickly. Otherwise, relax and keep a lid on it.

LET THE BARK GET DARK.

When smoked properly, ribs and large chunks of beef and pork should be enveloped in a dark mahogany, borderline black crust called "bark." This bark is the consequence of fat and spices sizzling with smoke on the surface of the meat developing into a caramelized crust. So before you take your dinner off the grill or wrap it in foil, make sure you've waited long enough for the delicious, dark bark to develop.

FEATURE THE STAR ATTRACTION.

The main ingredient in any smoked recipe is like the lead singer in a rock-and-roll band. Every other flavor should play a supporting role. In other words, don't upstage something inherently delicious with a potent marinade, heavy-handed seasonings, or thick coats of sauce. Harmonizing flavors in ways that feature the main ingredient is what separates the masters from the masses.

Appetizers

HICKORY SPICED MIXED NUTS

IDEAL
GRILL:

SMOKE INTENSITY: moderate

PREP TIME: 5 minutes

COOKING TIME: about 20 minutes

SPECIAL EQUIPMENT:
large disposable foil pan

SERVES: 4 (makes about 2 cups)

1 teaspoon packed light brown sugar
1 teaspoon ground cumin
¼ teaspoon ground cayenne pepper
2 cups salted mixed nuts *or*
   cocktail peanuts
2 teaspoons peanut oil

1 large handful hickory wood chips,
   soaked in water for at least 30 minutes

Use a pan that is large enough to spread all the nuts in a single layer so they are all exposed to smoke.

1 Prepare a two-zone fire for medium heat (350° to 450°F) (see pages 18–19).

2 In a large disposable foil pan mix the brown sugar, cumin, and cayenne pepper. Add the nuts and stir. Add the peanut oil, toss to coat, and set aside.

3 Brush the cooking grate clean. Drain and add the wood chips to the charcoal and put the lid on the grill. When the wood begins to smoke, cook the nuts over INDIRECT MEDIUM HEAT, with the lid closed, until they turn a shade or two darker and have developed a good smoky flavor, about 20 minutes. Wearing insulated barbecue mitts, remove the pan from the grill and let the nuts cool completely in the pan. They will crisp as they cool.

4 Serve at room temperature. Store any remaining nuts in an airtight container.

SMOKED FISH SPREAD
WITH CHÈVRE AND BRANDY

IDEAL GRILL:

SMOKE INTENSITY: moderate

PREP TIME: 30 minutes

COOKING TIME: about 18 minutes

COOLING TIME: 20 minutes

CHILLING TIME: at least 2 hours

SERVES: 12

- 1 pike perch, trout, *or* bluefish fillet (with skin), about 1 pound
- 2 tablespoons extra-virgin olive oil
  Kosher salt

- 1 large handful apple wood chips, soaked in water for at least 30 minutes

- 8 ounces chèvre *or* cream cheese, at room temperature
- ¼ cup (½ stick) unsalted butter, softened
- ¼ cup fresh lemon juice
- 2 tablespoons brandy
- 2 tablespoons minced shallots
- ½ teaspoon ground black pepper
- ⅛ teaspoon hot pepper sauce

- 1 tablespoon finely chopped fresh chives or Italian parsley leaves
  Sliced pumpernickel bread, toasted
  Whole-grain Dijon mustard

The fish can be smoked, stored in an airtight container, and refrigerated for one day.

1 Prepare a two-zone fire for medium-low heat (about 350°F) (see pages 18–19).

2 Brush the fillet on both sides with the oil and season the flesh evenly with ½ teaspoon salt.

3 Brush the cooking grate clean. Drain and add the wood chips to the charcoal and put the lid on the grill. When the wood begins to smoke, cook the fillet, flesh side down first, over DIRECT MEDIUM-LOW HEAT, with the lid closed, for 3 minutes. Turn the fillet, flesh side up, and move it over INDIRECT MEDIUM-LOW HEAT. Close the lid and cook until the flesh is opaque in the center, about 15 minutes. Remove from the grill and let cool for 20 minutes.

4 Remove and discard the skin from the fillet and cut the flesh into chunks. Place the chunks in a food processor fitted with a chopping blade. Add the cheese, butter, lemon juice, brandy, shallots, pepper, and hot pepper sauce. Process until smooth, scraping down the sides of the bowl once or twice. Season with salt. Transfer the spread to a bowl, cover, and refrigerate until chilled, at least 2 hours.

5 Just before serving, top with the chives. Serve chilled, with toasted pumpernickel and mustard.

After pureeing the smoked fish with the chèvre and other ingredients, be sure to chill the spread for at least two hours so that stronger flavors have time to meld with the subtler ones, creating a well-balanced overall taste.

TROUT AND ARTICHOKE DIP

IDEAL GRILL:

SMOKE INTENSITY: moderate

PREP TIME: 30 minutes

COOKING TIME: about 10 minutes

COOLING TIME: 1 hour

CHILLING TIME: at least 1 hour

SPECIAL EQUIPMENT: fish spatula

SERVINGS: 8 to 12

2 whole trout, each about 8 ounces,
   butterflied, not boned, heads removed
   Canola oil
   Kosher salt
   Ground black pepper

2 large handfuls mesquite wood chips,
   soaked in water for at least 30 minutes

1 can (14 ounces) artichoke hearts
   packed in water
½ cup mayonnaise
¼ cup sour cream
2 tablespoons minced fresh dill
2 tablespoons minced shallots
   Finely grated zest of 1 lemon
1 tablespoon fresh lemon juice
1 tablespoon white wine vinegar
½ teaspoon dried oregano
   Hot pepper sauce
   Crackers or crisp rye flat bread

1 Prepare a two-zone fire for medium heat (350° to 450°F) (see pages 18–19).

2 Brush the skin of the trout with oil and season the flesh lightly with salt and pepper.

3 Brush the cooking grate clean. Drain and add the wood chips to the charcoal and put the lid on the grill. When the wood begins to smoke, place the trout, opened and skin side down, over INDIRECT MEDIUM HEAT. Close the bottom vents, cover the grill, and cook until the flesh flakes when pierced with the tip of a knife, about 10 minutes. Using a fish spatula, transfer the trout to a cutting board and let cool to room temperature, about 1 hour.

4 Starting at the head end, lift and remove the backbone and any attached bones. Using a paring knife, remove any stray bones. Peel the skin off the flesh. Discard the skin and bones.

5 Drain the artichoke hearts in a fine mesh strainer and rinse under cold water. Squeeze the excess water from the artichokes (you should have about 1½ cups of artichokes). In a food processor pulse the artichokes until roughly chopped. Transfer to a serving bowl and gently mix in the trout, mayonnaise, sour cream, dill, shallots, lemon zest and juice, vinegar, and oregano. Season with salt and hot pepper sauce. Cover and refrigerate until chilled, at least 1 hour. (The dip can be refrigerated for up to 3 days.) Serve chilled with crackers.

The cooked trout cannot be picked up with tongs—it will fall apart. And a regular spatula is simply too small. Use a wide, large fish spatula to get the trout off the cooking grate and onto your cutting board.

CEDAR-PLANKED BRIE
WITH CHERRY CHUTNEY AND TOASTED ALMONDS

IDEAL
GRILL:

SMOKE INTENSITY: moderate

PREP TIME: 20 minutes

COOKING TIME: about 10 minutes

SPECIAL EQUIPMENT: 1 untreated cedar plank, 12 to 15 inches long and about 7 inches wide and ½ to ¾ inch thick, soaked in water for at least 1 hour

SERVES: 4 to 6

CHUTNEY

- 2 teaspoons vegetable oil
- 2 tablespoons minced yellow onion
- ½ teaspoon minced garlic
- 2 teaspoons peeled, minced fresh ginger
- ½ cup cherry preserves
  - Ground cinnamon
  - Crushed red pepper flakes

- 1 wheel (8 ounces) Brie cheese
- ¼ cup sliced almonds, toasted
  - Baguette slices *or* crackers

To toast the almonds, spread them on a baking sheet and bake in a preheated 350°F oven until golden brown and fragrant, about 10 minutes, stirring occasionally. Transfer to a plate to cool.

The cheese should be cool, no more than 10 minutes out of the refrigerator. If it's too warm, it will break and run all over the grill. Also, do not use overripe Brie, a wheel that is collapsing at its center. It, too, will break and run all over the grill.

1 In a small, heavy-bottomed saucepan over medium heat, warm the oil. Add the onion and cook, stirring often, until golden, about 5 minutes. Add the garlic and stir until fragrant, about 30 seconds. Stir in the ginger, preserves, a pinch of cinnamon, and a pinch of red pepper flakes and bring to a simmer. Reduce the heat to very low and cook for 3 minutes. Transfer to a bowl to cool.

2 Prepare a two-zone fire for medium heat (350° to 450°F) (see pages 18–19).

3 Brush the cooking grate clean. Place the soaked plank over DIRECT MEDIUM HEAT and close the lid. After 5 to 10 minutes, when the plank begins to smoke and char, turn the plank over.

4 Set the Brie in the center of the plank and cook over DIRECT MEDIUM HEAT, with the lid closed, until the cheese softens and the rind turns a pale golden brown, about 10 minutes. Use a wide spatula to transfer the Brie to a serving plate.

5 Spoon half of the chutney over the cheese and top with the toasted almonds. Serve with bread or crackers and the remaining chutney on the side.

CHILE CON QUESO

IDEAL GRILL:

SMOKE INTENSITY: strong

PREP TIME: 15 minutes

COOKING TIME: 30 minutes to 1 hour

SPECIAL EQUIPMENT:
10- to 12-inch cast-iron skillet

SERVES: 8 to 10

---

1 block (12 ounces) Monterey Jack cheese
1 block (12 ounces) mild or sharp cheddar cheese

4 mesquite wood chunks

SALSA
1 tablespoon extra-virgin olive oil
1 medium yellow onion, chopped
1 jalapeño chile pepper, seeded and finely chopped
1 large garlic clove, finely chopped
3 ripe plum tomatoes, seeded and diced
2 teaspoons dried Mexican oregano
  Kosher salt

1 tablespoon finely chopped fresh cilantro leaves
1 bag (12 ounces) tortilla chips

1 Prepare the smoker for indirect cooking with extremely low heat (about 175°F) (see pages 20–21).

2 In a 10- to 12-inch cast-iron skillet place the blocks of cheese side by side, about 2 inches apart.

3 Brush the cooking grate clean. Add the wood chunks to the charcoal and put the lid on the smoker. When smoke appears, place the skillet over **INDIRECT EXTREMELY LOW HEAT**, close the lid, and cook until the cheese has melted into two pools that run together, 30 minutes to 1 hour. Do not overcook or the cheese may separate.

4 Meanwhile, in a medium skillet over medium heat, heat the oil. Add the onion, jalapeño, and garlic and cook until the onion softens, about 3 minutes, stirring occasionally. Add the tomatoes and oregano and cook until the tomatoes give off their juices, about 5 minutes, stirring occasionally. Remove from the heat and season with salt.

5 Spoon the salsa over the melted cheese in the skillet and sprinkle with the cilantro. Serve warm with tortilla chips.

To turn the chile con queso into a main course, add a can of black or pinto beans, drained and rinsed, to the skillet with the tomatoes. Serve with warm flour tortillas, shredded lettuce, and thin red onion slices.

BARBECUED OYSTERS
WITH TOMATO-HORSERADISH SAUCE

IDEAL GRILL:

SMOKE INTENSITY: moderate

PREP TIME: 15 minutes, plus about 30 minutes to shuck the oysters

COOKING TIME: 2 to 4 minutes

SPECIAL EQUIPMENT: oyster knife

SERVES: 4

If you don't have an oyster knife, there is a common kitchen utensil that will also do the job—an old-fashioned bottle opener, the kind that has one pointed end and one blunt end. Wedge the pointed end, with the point facing up, into the small opening in the shell hinge. Holding the oyster secure with one hand, use the other hand to press down on the opener handle to act as a lever to pry the oyster shells apart. Use a paring knife to cut and loosen the oyster body from the shells.

SAUCE
- 2 teaspoons canola oil
- 1 scallion (white part only), finely chopped (reserve the green part)
- 2 tablespoons finely chopped celery
- 1 small garlic clove, minced
- 1 can (8 ounces) tomato sauce
- 1 tablespoon fresh lemon juice
- ½ teaspoon Worcestershire sauce
- 1 teaspoon prepared horseradish
- 1 teaspoon packed light brown sugar
  Hot pepper sauce

- 2 dozen large, fresh oysters
- 1 large handful cherry wood chips, soaked in water for at least 30 minutes

1 In a small saucepan over medium heat, heat the oil. Add the scallion (white part), celery, and garlic and cook until the celery softens, about 2 minutes, stirring occasionally. Add the tomato sauce, lemon juice, Worcestershire sauce, horseradish, and brown sugar and bring to a simmer. Reduce the heat to medium-low and simmer, uncovered, to blend the flavors, about 5 minutes, stirring occasionally. Remove from the heat. Season with hot pepper sauce.

2 Shuck the oysters: Grip each oyster, flat side up, in a folded kitchen towel. Find the small opening between the shells near the hinge and pry it open with an oyster knife. Try not to spill the delicious juices, known as the "oyster liquor," in the bottom of the shell. Cut the oyster meat loose from the top shell and then loosen the oyster from the bottom shell by running the oyster knife carefully under the body. Discard the top, flatter shell.

3 Prepare a two-zone fire for high heat (450° to 550°F) (see pages 18–19).

4 Spoon a generous teaspoon of the sauce on each oyster. Reserve the remaining sauce.

5 Brush the cooking grates clean. Drain and add the wood chips to the charcoal and put the lid on the grill. When the wood begins to smoke, cook the oysters, shell side down, over DIRECT HIGH HEAT, with the lid closed, until the sauce and oyster juices start to bubble and the edges of the oyster meat curl, 2 to 4 minutes. Using tongs, carefully remove the oysters from the grill. Finely chop the reserved green part of the scallion and scatter on top of the oysters. Serve with the remaining sauce.

SMOKED CHICKEN DRUMETTES
WITH ORANGE-HONEY GLAZE

IDEAL GRILL:

SMOKE INTENSITY: strong

PREP TIME: 15 minutes

COOKING TIME: 20 to 30 minutes

SERVES: 6 to 8

20 chicken drumettes, about
   3 pounds total
1 teaspoon kosher salt
½ teaspoon ground black pepper

GLAZE
½ cup orange marmalade
¼ cup honey
1 teaspoon kosher salt
1 teaspoon granulated garlic
1 teaspoon granulated onion
½ teaspoon ground cayenne pepper

2 large handfuls hickory wood chips,
  soaked in water for at least 30 minutes

1 Season the drumettes evenly with the salt and pepper.

2 Prepare a two-zone fire for medium heat (350° to 450°F) (see pages 18–19).

3 In a small, heavy-bottomed saucepan over medium heat, combine the glaze ingredients and stir until the marmalade melts, 5 to 6 minutes. Remove from the heat and cover to keep warm.

4 Brush the cooking grate clean. Drain and add the wood chips to the charcoal and put the lid on the grill. When the wood begins to smoke, cook the drumettes over INDIRECT MEDIUM HEAT, with the lid closed as much as possible, until the juices run clear and the meat is no longer pink at the bone, 20 to 30 minutes, turning and basting with the glaze two or three times during the final 10 to 12 minutes. Remove from the grill and serve warm.

Cooking the drumettes over indirect heat breaks down some of the chewy characteristics of the meat.

3

Red Meat

MESQUITE-GRILLED CHEESEBURGERS

WITH WARM CHIPOTLE SALSA

IDEAL
GRILL:

SMOKE INTENSITY: strong

PREP TIME: 20 minutes

COOKING TIME: 20 to 22 minutes

SERVES: 4

1½ pounds ground chuck (80% lean)
2 teaspoons ground cumin
1½ teaspoons ground black pepper
Kosher salt

2 tablespoons extra-virgin olive
oil, divided
1 small red onion, finely chopped
1 garlic clove, minced
4 plum tomatoes, each cut in
half lengthwise
2 large handfuls mesquite wood chips,
soaked in water for at least 30 minutes
3 tablespoons finely chopped fresh
cilantro leaves
1 canned chipotle chile pepper in
adobo sauce, minced
1 tablespoon fresh lime juice

4 slices smoked cheddar or smoked
Gouda cheese, each about 1 ounce
4 hamburger rolls

*For spicier salsa, add abobo sauce from
the canned chipotle chiles to taste.*

1 In a large bowl gently combine the ground chuck, cumin, pepper, and 1½ teaspoons salt. Shape into four patties of equal size, each about ¾ inch thick. With your thumb or the back of a spoon, make a shallow indentation about 1 inch wide in the center of each patty. This will help the patties cook evenly and prevent them from puffing on the grill. Cover and refrigerate until ready to cook.

2 Prepare a two-zone fire for high heat (450° to 550°F) (see pages 18–19).

3 In a medium skillet over medium heat, warm 1 tablespoon of the oil. Add the onion and garlic and cook until the onion is tender, about 3 minutes, stirring occasionally. Transfer to a medium bowl. Brush the tomatoes with the remaining 1 tablespoon of oil.

4 Brush the cooking grate clean. Drain and add half of the wood chips to the charcoal and put the lid on the grill. When smoke appears, place the tomato halves, cut side up, over INDIRECT HIGH HEAT. Close the lid and cook until the tomato juices are bubbling and the skins split, about 12 minutes. Remove from the grill. Remove and discard the tomato skins and roughly chop the tomatoes. Add the tomatoes, cilantro, chile, and lime juice to the onion mixture. Season with salt. Set aside.

5 Drain and add the remaining wood chips to the charcoal and put the lid on the grill. When the wood starts to smoke, cook the patties over DIRECT HIGH HEAT, with the lid closed as much as possible, until cooked to medium doneness, 8 to 10 minutes, turning once. During the last minute of cooking time, place a slice of cheese on each patty to melt and toast the rolls, cut side down. Remove from the grill and build each burger with the salsa. Serve warm.

LAMB CHEESEBURGERS

WITH MANCHEGO AND HARISSA

IDEAL
GRILL:

SMOKE INTENSITY: moderate

PREP TIME: 30 minutes

SOAKING TIME: 20 minutes

COOKING TIME: 8 to 10 minutes

SERVES: 6

HARISSA

 1 package (1½ ounces) dried New
    Mexico chiles, stems, seeds, and
    ribs removed
 ¾ cup boiling water
 2 medium garlic cloves,
    roughly chopped
1½ tablespoons extra-virgin olive oil
 1 tablespoon fresh lemon juice
 ½ teaspoon kosher salt
 ¼ teaspoon caraway seed
 ¼ teaspoon cumin seed
 ¼ teaspoon coriander seed

PATTIES

 2 pounds ground lamb
 ½ cup finely chopped fresh
    cilantro leaves
 2 teaspoons ground cumin
1½ teaspoons kosher salt
 ¾ teaspoon ground black pepper

 1 large handful oak wood chips, soaked
    in water for at least 30 minutes
 6 slices *manchego* cheese, each about
    1 ounce
 6 pita breads, tops cut off
 1 large tomato, cut into 6 slices
 6 leaves green lettuce
 6 slices red onion

Look for dried chiles that are pliable and fragrant.

1 Heat a large, heavy skillet over medium heat. Add the chiles, a few at a time, and cook until they turn a shade darker, about 20 seconds per side, using a wide metal spatula to press the chiles against the pan. Transfer to a heatproof bowl and let cool slightly. Roughly tear the chiles into 3-inch pieces. Add enough of the boiling water to cover the chiles and let them soak until softened, about 20 minutes.

2 Drain the chiles, reserving the soaking liquid. In a blender puree the chiles, garlic, oil, lemon juice, salt, caraway, cumin, and coriander seeds, and add enough of the soaking liquid as needed to make a smooth paste.

3 Prepare a two-zone fire for high heat (450° to 550°F) (see pages 18–19).

4 In a large bowl gently combine the patty ingredients and shape into six patties of equal size, each about ¾ inch thick. With your thumb or the back of a spoon, make a shallow indentation about 1 inch wide in the center of each patty. This will help the patties cook evenly and prevent them from puffing on the grill.

5 Brush the cooking grate clean. Drain and add the wood chips to the charcoal and put the lid on the grill. When smoke appears, cook the patties over DIRECT HIGH HEAT, with the lid closed as much as possible, until cooked to medium doneness, 8 to 10 minutes, turning them once when the patties release easily from the grate without sticking. During the last minute of cooking time, place a slice of cheese on each patty to melt and toast the pita breads. Serve each patty in a pita with a tomato slice, lettuce leaf, onion slice, and some *harissa*.

THREE-MEAT MEAT LOAF
WITH ROASTED PEPPER GLAZE

IDEAL GRILL:

SMOKE INTENSITY: strong

PREP TIME: 40 minutes

COOKING TIME: 1 to 1¼ hours

SPECIAL EQUIPMENT: large disposable foil pan, instant-read thermometer

SERVES: 6 to 8

Poblano chile peppers, sometimes called pasilla chiles, are on the mild side, although they do have some heat. They are elongated and have a shiny dark green color.

GLAZE
- 2 red bell peppers, about 10 ounces total
- 1 cup ketchup

MEAT LOAF
- 1 tablespoon extra-virgin olive oil
- 1 yellow onion, about 10 ounces, finely chopped
- 2 medium poblano chile peppers, about 8 ounces total, finely chopped
- 1 teaspoon minced garlic
- 1½ cups plain dry bread crumbs
- 1 large egg, beaten
- 3 tablespoons Worcestershire sauce
- 2 teaspoons kosher salt
- 1 teaspoon ground black pepper
- 1½ pounds ground beef (85% lean)
- ½ pound ground pork
- ½ pound ground veal

- 2 large handfuls mesquite wood chips, soaked in water for at least 30 minutes

Use a disposable foil pan, as smoke will discolor a solid metal pan.

1 Prepare a two-zone fire for medium heat (350° to 450°F) (see pages 18–19).

2 Brush the cooking grate clean. Grill the bell peppers over DIRECT MEDIUM HEAT, with the lid closed as much as possible, until blackened and blistered all over, 10 to 12 minutes, turning occasionally. Place the peppers in a bowl and cover with plastic wrap to trap the steam. Let stand for about 10 minutes. Remove and discard the charred skin, stem, and seeds.

3 In a blender or food processor puree the peppers until smooth. Add the ketchup and whirl until combined. Transfer to a bowl. Reserve ½ cup of the glaze to use in the meat loaf.

4 In a large skillet over medium heat, heat the oil. Add the onion, chile peppers, and garlic and cook until the onion is tender, about 5 minutes, stirring occasionally. Transfer the mixture to a large bowl and let cool. Add the ½ cup reserved glaze, the bread crumbs, egg, Worcestershire sauce, salt, and pepper to the onion mixture and stir to combine. Add the ground beef, pork, and veal. Using your hands, gently combine the meat loaf ingredients until well blended.

5 Divide the meat loaf mixture in half and form into two loaves, each about 4 inches wide by 6 to 7 inches long. Place the loaves in a large disposable foil pan.

6 At this point, check the temperature of the grill. If necessary, add enough lit or unlit briquettes to the charcoal to raise the temperature of the grill to 350° to 450°F. If using unlit briquettes, leave the grill lid off to help them light faster.

7 Drain and add one handful of the wood chips to the charcoal and put the lid on the grill. When the wood begins to smoke, cook the meat loaves in the pan over INDIRECT MEDIUM HEAT, with the lid closed, for 30 minutes. Brush the top of the loaves with ¼ cup of the glaze. Drain and add the remaining wood chips to the charcoal. Continue cooking until an instant-read thermometer inserted in the center of each loaf registers 165°F, 20 to 30 minutes more, rotating the pan once. Carefully transfer the pan to a heatproof surface and let rest for about 10 minutes.

8 Remove the loaves from the pan and cut into ½-inch slices. Serve warm with the remaining glaze.

MESQUITE SKIRT STEAK

WITH SALPICÓN SALAD

IDEAL GRILL:

SMOKE INTENSITY: moderate

PREP TIME: 30 minutes

COOKING TIME: 12 to 16 minutes

SERVES: 4

PASTE
- 2 tablespoons extra-virgin olive oil
- 2 tablespoons fresh lime juice
- 2 tablespoons pure chile powder
- 2 teaspoons ground cumin
- 1 teaspoon minced garlic
- 1 teaspoon kosher salt

1¾ pounds skirt steak, ½ to ¾ inch thick, trimmed of excess surface fat, cut into foot-long pieces

SALAD
- 1 pound very small red potatoes, scrubbed
- 2 ears fresh corn, husked
- 1 ripe Hass avocado, diced
- 4 medium radishes, thinly sliced
- 2 scallions (white and light green parts only), thinly sliced
- ¼ cup finely chopped fresh cilantro leaves
- 2 tablespoons fresh lime juice
- 1 canned chipotle chile pepper in adobo sauce, minced
- 1 garlic clove, minced
- ½ cup extra-virgin olive oil
  Kosher salt
  Ground black pepper

- 1 large handful mesquite wood chips, soaked in water for at least 30 minutes

  Flour tortillas (6 inches) (optional)

Skirt steak is typically well marbled with fat, which means it can be quite juicy and rich, but it can be chewy when it is undercooked, so cook until at least medium rare.

1 In a small bowl whisk the paste ingredients. Spread the paste on both sides of each steak. Set aside at room temperature for 15 to 30 minutes before cooking.

2 Put the potatoes in a medium saucepan and add salted water to cover. Bring to a boil over high heat. Reduce the heat to medium and cook the potatoes until tender when pierced with the tip of a knife, about 20 minutes. Drain, rinse under cold water, and drain again. Cut each potato in half, transfer to a medium bowl, and refrigerate to cool.

3 Prepare a two-zone fire for high heat (450° to 550°F) (see pages 18–19).

4 Brush the cooking grate clean. Cook the corn over DIRECT HIGH HEAT, with the lid closed as much as possible, until the kernels are brown in spots all over, 8 to 10 minutes, turning often. Remove from the grill and set aside. When the corn is cool enough to handle, cut the kernels from the cobs. Add to the bowl with the potatoes along with the avocado, radishes, scallions, and cilantro.

5 In a small bowl whisk the lime juice, chile, and garlic. Gradually whisk in the oil. Pour over the potato mixture and toss to combine. Season with salt and pepper. Refrigerate while cooking the steaks.

6 Drain and add the wood chips to the charcoal and put the lid on the grill. When smoke appears, cook the steaks over DIRECT HIGH HEAT, with the lid closed as much as possible, until cooked to your desired doneness, 4 to 6 minutes for medium rare, turning once or twice (if flare-ups occur, move the steaks temporarily over indirect heat). Remove from the grill and let rest for 3 to 5 minutes.

7 Cut the steaks across the grain into ½-inch slices. Serve immediately with the salad and warm tortillas, if desired.

SMOKED STEAK SALAD
WITH SESAME-GINGER DRESSING

IDEAL GRILL:

SMOKE INTENSITY: moderate

PREP TIME: 25 minutes

COOKING TIME: 8 to 10 minutes

SERVES: 4

RUB
- 2 teaspoons granulated garlic
- 1 teaspoon Chinese five spice
- 1 teaspoon ground black pepper
- 1 teaspoon ground coriander
- 1 teaspoon kosher salt

- 1 flank steak, 1½ to 2 pounds and about ¾ inch thick
  Peanut oil
- 2 portabello mushrooms, each about 4 ounces, stems and gills removed

DRESSING
- 3 tablespoons rice vinegar
- 2 tablespoons soy sauce
- 1 tablespoon toasted sesame oil
- 1 tablespoon peeled, minced fresh ginger
- 1 teaspoon toasted sesame seeds

- 2 large handfuls hickory wood chips, soaked in water for at least 30 minutes

SALAD
- 2 navel oranges
- 2 heads Boston lettuce *or* Bibb lettuce, about 1 pound total, separated into leaves
- ⅓ cup slivered almonds, toasted
- 4 scallions (white and light green parts only), thinly sliced

Flank steak has a terrific flavor, but it can be tough because of chewy fibers that run the length of the steak. Cut the steak across those fibers, perpendicular to the length of the steak, so you cut those fibers short and effectively make the meat tender.

1 In a small bowl combine the rub ingredients. Lightly brush the steak on both sides with peanut oil and season evenly with the rub. Allow the steak to stand at room temperature for 15 to 30 minutes before cooking.

2 Prepare a two-zone fire for medium heat (350° to 450°F) (see pages 18–19).

3 Generously brush each mushroom cap with peanut oil.

4 In a small bowl whisk the dressing ingredients, including 3 tablespoons peanut oil.

5 Brush the cooking grate clean. Drain and add the wood chips to the charcoal and put the lid on the grill. When the wood begins to smoke, cook the steak and mushrooms over DIRECT MEDIUM HEAT, with the bottom vents closed and the lid vent closed about halfway, until the steak is medium rare and the mushrooms are tender, turning once or twice. The steak will take 8 to 10 minutes (if flare-ups occur, move the steak temporarily over indirect heat) and the mushrooms will take 6 to 8 minutes. Remove from the grill and let the steak rest for 3 to 5 minutes.

6 Cut off a small slice from the top and bottom of each orange so the round fruit can stand upright. Use a serrated knife to cut the rind and white pith off the flesh in long arcs, starting at the top and following down along the natural curve of the fruit. Then hold the peeled fruit in your hand and use a paring knife to cut between the flesh and the white membranes separating the individual segments. Allow the segments to fall into a bowl. Discard the membranes, pith, and peel.

7 Cut the steak into thin strips and the mushrooms into bite-sized pieces. Divide the lettuce among plates and top with equal amounts of steak, mushrooms, oranges, almonds, and scallions. Drizzle generously with the dressing and serve right away.

To toast the almonds, spread them on a baking sheet and bake in a preheated 350°F oven until golden brown and fragrant, about 10 minutes, stirring occasionally. Transfer to a plate to cool.

OPEN-FACED STEAK SANDWICHES

WITH GREEN CHILE SALSA

IDEAL GRILL:

SMOKE INTENSITY: mild

PREP TIME: 30 minutes

COOKING TIME: 9 to 11 minutes

SERVES: 8

RUB

- 2 teaspoons granulated garlic
- 1 teaspoon kosher salt
- 1 teaspoon ground black pepper
- ¼ teaspoon ground cayenne pepper

- 2 flank steaks, each about 1 pound and
     ¾ inch thick
     Extra-virgin olive oil

SALSA

- 2 cups diced ripe plum tomatoes
- 4 scallions (white and light green parts
     only), thinly sliced
- 1 can (4 ounces) whole mild green
     chiles, drained, each chile cut into
     small dice
- 2 tablespoons finely chopped fresh
     cilantro leaves
- 1 tablespoon minced garlic
- 2 teaspoons red wine vinegar
- ½ teaspoon kosher salt
- ¼ teaspoon hot pepper sauce

- 8 slices rustic bread, each about
     ½ inch thick
- 2 large handfuls oak wood chips,
     soaked in water for at least 30 minutes

1 In a small bowl mix the rub ingredients. Lightly brush the steaks on both sides with oil and season evenly with the rub. Allow the steaks to stand at room temperature for 15 to 30 minutes before cooking.

2 Prepare a two-zone fire for medium heat (350° to 450°F) (see pages 18–19).

3 In a medium, nonreactive bowl mix the salsa ingredients and set aside at room temperature. Lightly brush the bread slices on both sides with oil.

4 Brush the cooking grates clean. Drain and add the wood chips to the charcoal and put the lid on the grill. When the wood begins to smoke, cook the steaks over DIRECT MEDIUM HEAT, with the lid closed as much as possible, until cooked to your desired doneness, 8 to 10 minutes for medium rare, turning once or twice (if flare-ups occur, move the steaks temporarily over indirect heat). Remove from the grill and let rest for 3 to 5 minutes. While the steaks rest, toast the bread over DIRECT MEDIUM HEAT for about 1 minute, turning once.

5 Cut the steaks across the grain into relatively thin slices and lay the slices on the toasted bread. Lightly top the steak with salsa and serve warm or at room temperature.

If you want to add even more flavor, rub the bread slices with a clove of garlic right after toasting them.

DIJON AND GARLIC RIB EYES
SMOKED WITH A LITTLE THYME

IDEAL GRILL:

SMOKE INTENSITY: mild

PREP TIME: 15 minutes

MARINATING TIME: 2 to 4 hours

COOKING TIME: 6 to 8 minutes

SERVES: 4 to 6

PASTE

1   small handful fresh thyme sprigs
3   tablespoons extra-virgin olive oil
1   tablespoon Dijon mustard
1   tablespoon balsamic vinegar
1   tablespoon minced garlic
½   teaspoon celery seed
    Kosher salt
    Ground black pepper

4   boneless rib eye steaks, each 12 to 16 ounces and about 1 inch thick
2   small handfuls hickory or mesquite wood chips, soaked in water for at least 30 minutes

To grill steaks evenly, make sure the charcoal extends at least four inches beyond the outer edge of each steak, and when you turn the steaks, swap their positions.

1   Strip the leaves from the thyme sprigs and reserve the sprigs for tossing on the coals later. Finely chop enough of the leaves to give you 2 tablespoons of chopped thyme. Mix the thyme leaves in a small bowl with the remaining paste ingredients, including 1 teaspoon salt and ¼ teaspoon pepper.

2   Brush the paste evenly over both sides of the steaks. Cover and refrigerate for 2 to 4 hours.

3   Remove the steaks from the refrigerator and season evenly with ½ teaspoon salt and ¼ teaspoon pepper. Allow the steaks to stand at room temperature for 15 to 30 minutes before cooking.

4   Prepare a two-zone fire for high heat (450° to 550°F) (see pages 18–19).

5   Brush the cooking grate clean. Drain and add the wood chips and thyme sprigs to the charcoal and put the lid on the grill. When smoke appears, grill the steaks over DIRECT HIGH HEAT, with the lid closed as much as possible, until cooked to your desired doneness, 6 to 8 minutes for medium rare, turning once or twice (if flare-ups occur, move the steaks temporarily over indirect heat). Remove from the grill and let rest for 3 to 5 minutes. Serve warm.

PECAN-SMOKED VEAL CHOPS
WITH SAUTÉED LEEK AND MUSHROOMS

IDEAL GRILL:

SMOKE INTENSITY: **strong**

PREP TIME: **20 minutes**

COOKING TIME: **6 to 8 minutes**

SERVES: **4**

The wet tarragon paste is truly delicious, but all that moisture prevents browning, so start searing the chops on at least one side first, and then begin brushing with the paste.

PASTE
- ¼ cup finely chopped fresh tarragon leaves
- 2 tablespoons whole-grain mustard
- 2 tablespoons toasted hazelnut oil *or* walnut oil *or* extra-virgin olive oil
- 2 tablespoons dry white wine *or* dry vermouth

- 4 veal rib chops, each about 12 ounces and 1 inch thick
- 1 tablespoon vegetable oil
  Kosher salt
  Ground black pepper

- 1 large handful pecan wood chips, soaked in water for at least 30 minutes

- 4 tablespoons (½ stick) unsalted butter, divided
- 1 small leek (white and light green parts only), washed well to remove any dirt, thinly sliced
- 1 pound shiitake mushrooms, stems removed, caps thinly sliced
- ¼ cup dry white wine *or* dry vermouth
- 1 teaspoon whole-grain mustard

1 In a small bowl mix the paste ingredients.

2 Lightly brush the veal chops on both sides with the vegetable oil and season evenly with 2 teaspoons salt and ½ teaspoon pepper. Allow the chops to stand at room temperature for 15 to 30 minutes before cooking.

3 Prepare a two-zone fire for medium heat (350° to 450°F) (see pages 18–19).

4 Brush the cooking grate clean. Drain and add the wood chips to the charcoal and put the lid on the grill. When the wood begins to smoke, place the chops over DIRECT MEDIUM HEAT. Brush the tops of the chops with half of the paste, put the lid on the grill, and cook for 3 to 4 minutes. Turn the chops over and brush them with the remaining paste. Continue to cook until the chops are slightly pink in the center, 3 to 4 minutes more. Remove from the grill and let rest while you prepare the leek and mushrooms.

5 In a large skillet over medium heat, melt 2 tablespoons of the butter. Add the leek and cook until softened, about 2 minutes. Add the mushrooms and cook until they are dry, about 3 minutes, stirring occasionally. Pour in the wine and bring to a boil. Remove from the heat. Add the remaining 2 tablespoons butter and the mustard. Using a wooden spoon, stir until the butter emulsifies into a creamy sauce. Season with salt and pepper. Top the chops with the leek, mushrooms, and sauce and serve right away.

MOROCCAN SMOKE-ROASTED BEEF TENDERLOIN

IDEAL GRILL:

SMOKE INTENSITY: moderate

PREP TIME: 20 minutes

COOKING TIME: about 42 minutes

SPECIAL EQUIPMENT:
spice mill or mortar and pestle,
butcher's twine, large disposable
foil pan, instant-read thermometer

SERVES: 6 to 8

RUB
1½ teaspoons caraway seed
1½ teaspoons coriander seed
1½ teaspoons cumin seed
1½ teaspoons packed dark brown sugar,
    preferably *muscovado*
 1 teaspoon kosher salt
¼ teaspoon ground cinnamon
¼ teaspoon ground black pepper
⅛ teaspoon ground cloves

 1 beef tenderloin roast, about 3
    pounds, preferably from the thicker
    chateaubriand end, trimmed of silver
    skin and excess fat
 2 tablespoons extra-virgin olive oil
 2 large handfuls mesquite wood chips,
    soaked in water for at least 30 minutes

*The larger end of the tenderloin,
sometimes called the "chateaubriand,"
is a better cut for this grilling method.
Its thicker diameter assures more even
cooking without the meat drying out.*

Sear the tenderloin when the coals reach the high end of the medium heat temperature range, 450°F. By the time the roast is seared over direct heat, the temperature of the grill will be in the middle of the range and ready to continue cooking with indirect heat.

1 In a spice mill or mortar and pestle coarsely grind the caraway, coriander, and cumin seeds (or crush the seeds on a cutting board under a heavy saucepan). Pour into a small bowl and mix in the remaining rub ingredients.

2 Tie the roast with butcher's twine every couple of inches to make it even and compact. Lightly coat the roast with the oil and season evenly with the rub. Allow the roast to stand at room temperature for 15 to 30 minutes before cooking.

3 Prepare a two-zone fire for medium-high heat (400° to 500°F) (see pages 18–19). Place a large disposable foil pan beside the bed of charcoal and fill three-quarters of the way full with water.

4 Brush the cooking grate clean. Sear the roast over DIRECT MEDIUM-HIGH HEAT, with the lid closed as much as possible, for about 12 minutes, turning a quarter turn once every 3 to 4 minutes.

5 Slide the roast over INDIRECT MEDIUM-HIGH HEAT, directly over the foil pan. Drain and add the wood chips to the charcoal. Close the lid and cook until an instant-read thermometer inserted into the center of the thickest part of the roast registers 125°F for medium rare, about 30 minutes. Transfer to a cutting board and let rest for 10 to 15 minutes (the internal temperature will rise 5 to 10 degrees during this time).

6 Remove the twine and cut the roast crosswise into ½-inch slices. Serve warm.

PEPPERY BEEF JERKY

IDEAL GRILL:

SMOKE INTENSITY: moderate

FREEZING TIME: 1 to 2 hours

MARINATING TIME: 1 hour

COOKING TIME: 6 to 7 hours

SPECIAL EQUIPMENT:
mortar and pestle

SERVES: 12

1 eye of round beef roast, about
2 pounds, silver skin and external
fat removed

MARINADE
¼ cup soy sauce
2 tablespoons Worcestershire sauce
1 tablespoon honey

RUB
2 teaspoons black peppercorns
2 teaspoons green peppercorns
2 teaspoons pink peppercorns
2 teaspoons white peppercorns
2 teaspoons Sichuan peppercorns

1 large handful hickory wood chunks

Smoking raw meats at temperatures below 225°F can cause bacterial growth. To avoid that risk, the USDA recommends steaming or roasting meats for jerky to 160°F before smoking them.

Once the initial smoke wears off, you need no more. The rest of the cooking is simply about drying out the meat.

1 Freeze the roast until frosty but not hard, 1 to 2 hours. Place the roast on a cutting board with the flat end facing right or left, depending on your dominant hand. Starting at the flat end, cut off ¼-inch-thick slices.

2 In a large bowl whisk the marinade ingredients until thoroughly blended. Add the beef slices and turn to coat. Refrigerate, uncovered, for 1 hour.

3 Meanwhile, coarsely crush the peppercorns using a mortar and pestle (or crush them on a cutting board under a heavy saucepan). Pour into a small bowl and mix thoroughly.

4 Remove the beef slices from the bowl and spread them out flat on a large sheet pan. Discard the marinade. Season the slices evenly with half of the rub, pressing the pepper into the meat. Turn the slices over and repeat.

5 Prepare the smoker for indirect cooking with extremely low heat (about 175°F) (see pages 20–21). Use only about one-half of a chimney starter full of charcoal briquettes.

6 Brush the cooking grate clean. Add the wood chunks to the charcoal. Smoke the beef slices over INDIRECT EXTREMELY LOW HEAT, with the lid closed, until they are dry and almost brittle, 6 to 7 hours. Add lit briquettes (the heat is too low in the smoker to ignite unlit briquettes) to the charcoal to keep the heat low and even. Transfer the jerky to a platter and let cool.

7 Serve within 2 hours of removing from the smoker. Store leftovers in an airtight container in the refrigerator for up to 2 weeks, or wrap airtight and freeze for up to 4 months.

SPICED AND SMOKED CHUCK ROAST

IDEAL
GRILL:

SMOKE INTENSITY: moderate

PREP TIME: 15 minutes, plus about
25 minutes for the sauce

BRAISING TIME: about 2 hours

COOLING TIME: about 4 hours

COOKING TIME: about 1 hour

SPECIAL EQUIPMENT: large disposable
foil pan, instant-read thermometer

SERVES: 6

BRAISING LIQUID

3½ quarts water
 2 tablespoons coriander seed
 2 tablespoons black peppercorns
 1 tablespoon cardamom pods
 1 tablespoon kosher salt
 2 whole star anise
 1 cinnamon stick

 1 boneless beef chuck roast, about
    3¾ pounds, rolled and tied

SAUCE

 1 tablespoon vegetable oil
 1 small yellow onion, finely chopped
 2 tablespoons peeled, minced
    fresh ginger
 2 teaspoons minced garlic
 1 cup ketchup
 1 cup ketchup-style chili sauce *or*
    bottled barbecue sauce
 ½ cup sherry vinegar *or* cider vinegar
 ½ cup packed light brown sugar
 ⅓ cup water
 ⅓ cup whole-grain mustard
 ⅛ teaspoon hot pepper sauce

 2 large handfuls mesquite wood chips,
    soaked in water for at least 30 minutes

The roast can be covered and refrigerated for up to one day after braising and cooling. Let stand at room temperature for one hour before cooking.

1 In a large stockpot over high heat, bring the braising liquid ingredients to a boil. Add the roast and add more water to cover, if needed. Return to a boil and reduce the heat to medium-low. Cover and simmer the roast until the internal temperature reaches 185°F, about 2 hours.

2 Transfer the roast to a platter and discard the braising liquid. Let stand at room temperature until cooled, about 2 hours. Wrap the roast in plastic wrap and refrigerate until chilled, at least 2 hours. Meanwhile, make the sauce.

3 In a medium saucepan over medium heat, warm the oil. Add the onion, ginger, and garlic and cook until the onion is tender, about 3 minutes, stirring often. Add the remaining sauce ingredients and bring to a simmer. Reduce the heat to medium-low and cook until thickened, about 20 minutes, stirring often. Remove from the heat and let the sauce cool.

4 Prepare a two-zone fire for low heat (250° to 350°F) (see pages 18–19). Place a large disposable foil pan beside the bed of charcoal and fill three-quarters of the way full with water. Maintain the temperature between 325° to 350°F.

5 Brush the cooking grate clean. Drain and add one handful of the wood chips to the charcoal and put the lid on the grill. When the wood begins to smoke, cook the roast over INDIRECT LOW HEAT, with the lid closed, for 30 minutes. Drain and add the remaining wood chips to the charcoal and continue cooking over INDIRECT LOW HEAT, with the lid closed, until the meat is heated through and the internal temperature reaches 140°F, about 30 minutes more. During the last 10 minutes, brush the roast with some of the sauce. Transfer to a cutting board, tent with aluminum foil, and let rest for about 10 minutes (the internal temperature will rise 5 to 10 degrees during this time).

6 Cut the roast against the grain into thin slices. Serve with the remaining sauce and white bread, if desired. Serving suggestion: Classic Coleslaw (for the recipe, see page 181).

SMOKY BRAISED BEEF CHILI

IDEAL GRILL:

SMOKE INTENSITY: moderate

PREP TIME: 30 minutes

COOKING TIME: about 2¼ hours

SPECIAL EQUIPMENT:
large pot suitable for the grill

SERVES: 6

If you like beans in your chili, by all means add them. Two 15½-ounce cans of pinto or pink beans, rinsed, added to the pot during the last 15 minutes of cooking, will make a very thick chili.

2   boneless beef chuck roasts, each about 2 pounds
3   tablespoons extra-virgin olive oil, divided
    Kosher salt
    Ground black pepper

4   mesquite wood chunks

2   medium yellow onions, roughly chopped
2   bell peppers, 1 green and 1 red, cut into ½-inch dice
4   medium garlic cloves, minced
1   serrano chile pepper, seeded and minced
¼   cup prepared chili powder
2   teaspoons dried oregano
2   teaspoons ground cumin
1   can (28 ounces) plum tomatoes in juice, roughly chopped
1   bottle (12 fluid ounces) dark beer (not stout)

1   Prepare a two-zone fire for high heat (450° to 550°F) (see pages 18–19).

2   Cut each roast in half. Brush with 1 tablespoon of the oil and season evenly with 1½ teaspoons salt and ¾ teaspoon pepper. Allow the roasts to stand at room temperature for 15 to 30 minutes before cooking.

3   Brush the cooking grate clean. Add two wood chunks to the charcoal and put the lid on the grill. When the wood begins to smoke, cook the roasts over DIRECT HIGH HEAT, with the lid closed as much as possible, until browned on both sides, about 6 minutes, turning once. Move the roasts over INDIRECT HIGH HEAT and continue cooking while you cook the vegetables.

4   In a large pot suitable for the grill combine the remaining 2 tablespoons oil with the onions, bell peppers, garlic, and chile. Cook over DIRECT HIGH HEAT, with the lid closed as much as possible, until the onions are tender, 8 to 10 minutes, stirring occasionally. Add the chili powder, oregano, and cumin and stir well. Stir in the tomatoes with their juice and the beer. Transfer the roasts to the pot and bring the mixture to a simmer. Cover the pot with its lid or cover tightly with aluminum foil. By this time, the coals should have burned down to about 350°F. Move the pot over INDIRECT MEDIUM HEAT, close the lid, and cook until the meat is so tender it falls apart, about 2 hours. After 1 hour, add more lit briquettes to maintain the heat and add the two remaining wood chunks to the charcoal. Remove the pot from the grill, remove the lid, and let rest for about 5 minutes. Skim off any fat from the surface. Using two forks, pull the meat into bite-sized pieces. Season with salt and pepper. Serve hot.

KOREAN TRI-TIP
WITH QUICK PICKLED VEGETABLES

IDEAL GRILL:

SMOKE INTENSITY: moderate

PREP TIME: 30 minutes

MARINATING TIME: 8 to 24 hours

COOKING TIME: 23 to 30 minutes

SERVES: 4

Tri-tip is a triangular cut of beef from the bottom sirloin. It looks like a small roast or a thick steak. If you have trouble finding tri-tip you can use any thick steak, such as London broil, for this recipe.

MARINADE

- 1 Asian pear, about 8 ounces, coarsely grated
- ½ cup thinly sliced scallions (white and light green parts only)
- ¼ cup dry sherry
- ¼ cup soy sauce
- 2 tablespoons packed light brown sugar
- 1½ tablespoons roughly chopped garlic
- 1 tablespoon sesame seeds
- 1 tablespoon toasted sesame oil
- ½ teaspoon crushed red pepper flakes

- 1 tri-tip roast, 1½ to 2 pounds, excess fat and silver skin removed

VEGETABLES

- ⅓ cup rice vinegar
- 1 tablespoon granulated sugar
- 2 teaspoons kosher salt
- 2 carrots, about 6 ounces total, julienned
- 1 piece daikon, about 6 ounces, julienned

- 1 large handful oak or apple wood chips, soaked in water for at least 30 minutes

1 In a medium bowl whisk the marinade ingredients until the sugar is dissolved. Place the roast in a large, resealable plastic bag and pour in the marinade. Press the air out of the bag and seal tightly. Turn the bag to distribute the marinade and refrigerate for 8 to 24 hours, turning once or twice. Allow the roast to stand at room temperature for about 30 minutes before cooking.

2 In a medium bowl whisk the vinegar, sugar, and salt. Add the carrots and daikon and toss to coat. Cover and let stand at room temperature for at least 30 minutes or up to 2 hours. Drain the vegetables just before serving.

3 Prepare a two-zone fire for medium heat (350° to 450°F) (see pages 18–19).

4 Remove the roast from the bag and discard the marinade. Brush the cooking grate clean. Drain and add the wood chips to the charcoal and put the lid on the grill. When the wood begins to smoke, cook the roast over DIRECT MEDIUM HEAT, with the lid closed as much as possible, until well marked on both sides, 8 to 10 minutes, turning once or twice. Then move the roast over INDIRECT MEDIUM HEAT, close the lid, and continue cooking until it reaches your desired doneness, 15 to 20 minutes for medium rare. Remove from the grill and let rest for 5 to 10 minutes.

5 Cut the roast across the grain into thin slices. Serve warm with the pickled vegetables on the side.

SLOW-SMOKED MESQUITE BRISKET

IDEAL
GRILL:

SMOKE INTENSITY: strong

PREP TIME: 45 minutes

MARINATING TIME: 12 to 24 hours

COOKING TIME: 7 to 9 hours

RESTING TIME: 1 to 2 hours

SPECIAL EQUIPMENT: food syringe;
extra-large disposable foil roasting
pan; instant-read thermometer

SERVINGS: 12 to 15

1   whole, untrimmed beef brisket,
    including both the flat and point
    sections, 10 to 12 pounds, preferably
    the *Certified Angus Beef*® brand
1   cup low-sodium beef broth
⅓   cup yellow mustard

RUB
2   tablespoons ancho chile powder
1   tablespoon packed light brown sugar
1   tablespoon kosher salt
1   tablespoon onion powder
1   tablespoon paprika
1   tablespoon ground cumin
2   teaspoons ground black pepper
2   teaspoons ground allspice

8   fist-sized mesquite wood chunks

*Plan on a full day of cooking time.
Yes, it takes time to make that cut of meat
tender and delicious. For this big piece
of meat, you will need a big smoker. A
22½-inch-diameter Smokey Mountain
Cooker™ smoker works very well for this,
but the 18-inch version is too small.*

*Plan ahead. First you will need to find and purchase a very large piece of meat, at least
10 to 12 pounds, which you might need to buy from a specialty meat market or special-order
from a supermarket. The quality of the meat is the most important part of the recipe. Do not
try to barbecue a low-quality brisket; it will be tough and dry. Buy a top-quality brisket from
a reputable brand, such as the Certified Angus Beef® brand. You need a full, untrimmed
brisket that includes a flat, relatively lean section (called "the flat") and a thicker, fattier
section (called "the point"). When you lift the brisket up from the point end, the flat should
flop over easily, indicating there is not too much connective tissue making the meat tight
and tough.*

1 The night before you smoke the brisket, trim it. Using a very sharp knife on the fat side,
   trim the fat so that it is about ⅓ inch thick, but no less. On the meatier side, remove the
   web-like membrane that covers the meat, so that you can clearly see (and eventually season)
   the coarsely grained meat underneath. Then, using a food syringe, inject the meat with the
   beef broth: With the fat side facing down in an extra-large foil roasting pan, imagine the
   brisket in 1-inch squares and inject each square with some of the broth, inserting the needle
   parallel to the grain of the meat and slowly pulling the needle out as you inject the broth
   (see photo on facing page). Some broth will seep out, but try to keep as much as possible
   inside the meat. Then smear the mustard over both sides of the brisket.

2 In a small bowl mix the rub ingredients. Massage the rub all over the brisket creating a
   paste with the mustard and broth. Turn the brisket so that the fat side is facing up. Cover
   the pan and refrigerate for at least 12 hours or up to 24 hours. Remove the brisket from
   the refrigerator and let stand in the pan at room temperature for 1 hour before smoking.

3 Prepare the smoker for indirect cooking with very low heat (200° to 250°F) (see pages 20–21).

4 Add two wood chunks to the charcoal. Smoke the brisket in the pan over INDIRECT VERY
   LOW HEAT, with the lid closed, for 4 hours, adjusting the vents so the temperature inside
   the smoker stays as close to 225°F as possible. At the start of the second, third, and fourth
   hours, add two more wood chunks to the charcoal and baste the brisket with any liquid that
   accumulates in the pan.

5 After 4 hours, use an instant-read thermometer to check the internal temperature of the
   meat. If it has not reached 160°F, continue cooking until it does. If it has reached 160°F,
   remove the brisket in the pan from the smoker. Put the lid back on the smoker to prevent
   heat loss. Add more lit briquettes and refill the water pan to maintain the 225°F temperature.

6 On a large work surface, lay out three sheets of heavy-duty aluminum foil, each about
   3 feet long, overlapping the sheets slightly along their longer sides. Place the brisket in
   the center of the foil, fat side up. Pour ½ cup of the liquid in the pan over the meat, and fold
   up the edges to wrap the brisket tightly to trap the steam. At this point you can discard the
   remaining liquid that has accumulated in the pan, though some people like to save it for
   adding to their barbecue sauce.

With the needle running parallel to the grain of the meat, inject the broth as evenly as you can. As you press the plunger, slowly draw the needle to the surface of the meat, and then insert the needle in a nearby spot.

7 Return the brisket to the pan, fat side facing up, and return the pan to the smoker. Cook over **INDIRECT VERY LOW HEAT**, with the lid closed, until the meat is so tender that when you insert the probe of an instant-read thermometer and push it back and forth, it easily tears the meat, at least 3 hours and as long as 5 hours. The internal temperature should be 190° to 195°F, though tenderness is a more important indicator of doneness than the temperature. The amount of time required will depend on the particular breed and other characteristics of the meat. Remove from the smoker and let the brisket rest at room temperature for 1 to 2 hours.

8 Unwrap the brisket and cut across the grain into thin slices. Serve warm with your favorite barbecue sauce and side dishes, such as Cider and Bacon Beans (for the recipe, see page 175). If you have any leftover brisket, use it to make Barbecued Brisket Tamales (for the recipe, see page 73).

BARBECUED BRISKET TAMALES

PREP TIME: 1 hour

STEAMING TIME: 1½ hours

SPECIAL EQUIPMENT: stand mixer, tall stockpot, large steamer insert

SERVES: 12

SAUCE

- 2 tablespoons extra-virgin olive oil
- ⅓ cup finely chopped red onion
- 1 tablespoon minced garlic
- 1 cup canned crushed tomatoes
- 1 cup amber Mexican beer
- 2 dried *pasilla* chiles, stemmed, seeded, and cut into strips
- 1 tablespoon cider vinegar
- 1 teaspoon dried oregano
- 1 teaspoon ground cumin
- ½ teaspoon kosher salt

- 1 package (3 ounces) dried corn husks for tamales (48 husks)

- 3 cups smoked, shredded brisket (for the recipe, see page 70)

- 5 cups instant masa harina
- 2 teaspoons baking powder
- 2 teaspoons kosher salt
- 4 cups warm water
- 1⅓ cups melted lard
  Sour cream
  Chopped fresh cilantro leaves

To be on the safe side, soak extra corn husks. Some will tear, some will not be big enough, and some can be used to patch holes in the husks you're using. There are about 48 husks in a standard three-ounce bag, so just soak them all.

1 In a medium, heavy-bottomed saucepan over medium heat, warm the oil. Add the onion and cook until softened, about 3 minutes, stirring occasionally. Add the garlic and cook until golden, about 2 minutes. Stir in the remaining sauce ingredients and bring to a boil. Reduce the heat to medium-low and simmer, uncovered, until slightly thickened, about 20 minutes, stirring often. Remove from the heat and cover. Let stand for 15 minutes to soften the chiles. Puree in a blender or with an immersion blender.

2 Set the corn husks in a tall stockpot. Cover them with boiling water. Set a small plate on top of the husks to keep them submerged in the water. Steep until softened, about 30 minutes.

3 In a food processor fitted with the metal chopping blade pulse the shredded brisket until coarsely ground. Scrape into a large bowl, add ¾ cup of the sauce (reserve the remaining sauce for serving), and stir until well combined.

4 In the bowl of a stand mixer combine the masa harina, baking powder, and salt. Add the water and lard, then stir and beat with the paddle attachment on low speed to make a firm, spongy dough.

5 Drain the husks well. Tear a couple of the husks lengthwise to make 40 thin strips for tying the folded tamales. For each tamale, place a husk on the work surface, curved side facing up with the pointed end facing away from you. Spread about 3 generous tablespoons of the masa dough into the center of the husk; smear the dough into a rough rectangle about 4 inches wide by 3 inches long, leaving a border at the longer edge of the husk. Spoon 1 to 2 tablespoons of the brisket mixture in a line down the center of the dough. Bring the two long sides of the husk together to enclose the brisket filling with the masa, and pinch the seam closed. Wrap the tamale in the husk. Fold the pointed end of the husk up. Using a husk strip, tie and secure the folded husk in place, leaving the top of the tamale open (see photo at bottom left).

6 Set up a large steamer insert or a steaming basket in a tall stockpot. Add enough water to almost reach, but not touch, the bottom of the steamer. Stand the tamales, open ends up, on the steamer. (The tamales should support each other to stand, but not be packed together.) Cover the pot tightly and bring the water to a boil over high heat. Reduce the heat to medium-low to maintain a steady head of steam in the pot. Steam until the tamale dough has lost its raw look and taste and is firm enough to easily pull away from the husk, about 1½ hours. Add more hot water to the pot as needed.

7 Reheat the reserved sauce and transfer to a serving bowl. Serve the tamales warm with the sauce, sour cream, and cilantro.

Any smoked meat will work in this recipe. Next time try chicken or pork.

PECAN-SMOKED LAMB SHOULDER

WITH VEGETABLE COUSCOUS

IDEAL GRILL:

SMOKE INTENSITY: moderate

PREP TIME: 30 minutes

REFRIGERATION TIME:
12 to 24 hours

COOKING TIME: about 2¼ hours

SPECIAL EQUIPMENT: butcher's twine,
instant-read thermometer

SERVES: 6

PASTE

¼ cup extra-virgin olive oil
¼ cup fresh thyme leaves
4 garlic cloves, finely chopped
1½ teaspoons crushed red pepper flakes
1 teaspoon kosher salt
½ teaspoon ground black pepper

1 boneless lamb shoulder, about
  3½ pounds, trimmed of excess fat

2 large handfuls pecan wood chips,
  soaked in water for at least 30 minutes

2 tablespoons unsalted butter
4 medium scallions (white and light
  green parts only), thinly sliced
1 medium red bell pepper, finely diced
1 small zucchini, ends trimmed,
  finely diced
2 teaspoons finely chopped fresh
  oregano leaves *or* 1 teaspoon
  dried oregano
1 teaspoon paprika
¾ teaspoon kosher salt
½ teaspoon ground black pepper
3 cups low-sodium chicken broth
1½ cups quick-cooking couscous

1 In a food processor combine the paste ingredients and process until smooth.

2 Place the lamb, smooth side down, on a work surface. Spread the paste in a thick layer over the rough side (the side that faced the bone) of the lamb. Starting at a long end, roll the lamb into a thick cylinder. Tie with butcher's twine to hold its shape. Place in a large, resealable plastic bag and refrigerate for 12 to 24 hours.

3 Prepare the grill for indirect cooking over medium heat (350° to 450°F) (see pages 22–23).

4 Remove the lamb from the bag. Brush the cooking grates clean. Drain and add one handful of the wood chips to the smoker box of a gas grill, following manufacturer's instructions, and close the lid. When the wood begins to smoke, cook the lamb over INDIRECT MEDIUM HEAT, with the lid closed, for 1 hour. After the first hour, drain and add the remaining wood chips to the smoker box. Close the lid and continue to cook until the internal temperature reaches 155°F, about 1¼ hours longer. Remove from the grill and wrap tightly in aluminum foil. Let the lamb rest for 10 to 15 minutes (the internal temperature will rise 5 to 10 degrees during this time). While the lamb is resting, make the couscous.

5 In a large saucepan over medium heat, melt the butter. Add the scallions, bell pepper, and zucchini and cook until slightly softened, about 4 minutes, stirring often. Stir in the oregano, paprika, salt, and pepper. Add the broth and bring to a boil over high heat. Stir in the couscous. Remove from the heat and cover tightly. Let stand until the liquid has been absorbed, about 5 minutes. Fluff the couscous with a fork.

6 Unwrap the lamb, remove the twine, and cut across the grain into slices. Spoon the couscous onto dinner plates, and top with the lamb and the carving juices.

Use the paste in this recipe to season a boneless leg of lamb, about 4½ pounds, and cook according to the directions for the recipe on page 77.

RED MEAT

OAK-ROASTED LEG OF LAMB

WITH HAZELNUT GREMOLATA

IDEAL GRILL:

SMOKE INTENSITY: moderate

PREP TIME: 30 minutes

COOKING TIME: about 1 hour

SPECIAL EQUIPMENT:
butcher's twine, large disposable foil pan, instant-read thermometer

SERVES: 8

GREMOLATA
- ⅔ cup hazelnuts
- 2 medium garlic cloves
- 1 cup tightly packed fresh Italian parsley leaves and tender stems
  Finely grated zest of 2 medium lemons
  Kosher salt
  Ground black pepper

- 1 boneless leg of lamb, about 4½ pounds, trimmed of any excess fat and sinew, butterflied
  Extra-virgin olive oil
- 2 large handfuls oak wood chips, soaked in water for at least 30 minutes

🔥 *Grapevines would be an excellent alternative for the oak wood chips.*

1 Preheat the oven to 350°F. Spread the hazelnuts on a rimmed baking sheet. Bake until the skins are cracked, about 10 minutes, stirring occasionally. Transfer to a clean kitchen towel and let cool for 10 minutes. Wrap and rub the cooled nuts in the towel to remove the skins (some skin will remain); roughly chop them.

2 In a food processor mince the garlic. Add the hazelnuts, parsley, lemon zest, ½ teaspoon salt, and ½ teaspoon pepper. Pulse into a coarse paste.

3 Place the lamb, cut side up, on a work surface. Using a sharp knife, make angled, deep cuts in the thickest parts of the meat, taking care not to cut all the way through, and spread the flaps open like a book. When you are finished, the lamb should be about ¾ inch thick. Spread the gremolata evenly over the cut surface of the lamb. Starting at a short end, roll up the lamb. Tie the roll crosswise in several places with butcher's twine. Brush the outside of the lamb with oil and season evenly with 1 teaspoon salt and ½ teaspoon pepper. Set aside at room temperature while you prepare the grill.

4 Prepare a two-zone fire for medium heat (350° to 450°F) (see pages 18–19). Place a large disposable foil pan beside the bed of charcoal and fill three-quarters of the way full with water.

5 Brush the cooking grate clean. Sear the lamb over DIRECT MEDIUM HEAT, with the lid closed as much as possible, until nicely browned on all sides, about 12 minutes, turning occasionally.

6 Drain half of the wood chips and add them to the charcoal. Set the lamb over the foil pan and put the lid on the grill. Grill over INDIRECT MEDIUM HEAT for 30 minutes. Drain and add the remaining wood chips to the charcoal. If necessary, add more lit charcoal to maintain the temperature. Cover and continue cooking until an instant-read thermometer inserted in the thickest part of the lamb reaches 130°F for medium rare, about 20 minutes.

7 Transfer the lamb to a cutting board and let rest for 10 to 15 minutes (the internal temperature will rise 5 to 10 degrees during this time). Cut the lamb crosswise into ½-inch-thick slices. Remove the twine and serve warm.

🔥 *Do not untie the lamb before carving. The butcher's twine will keep the roast secure, the better to cut even slices.*

ANCHO-MARINATED LEG OF LAMB

WITH TOMATO-CUCUMBER SALSA

IDEAL GRILL:

SMOKE INTENSITY: moderate

PREP TIME: 30 minutes

MARINATING TIME: 12 to 24 hours

DRAINING TIME: 1 hour

COOKING TIME: about 1½ hours

SPECIAL EQUIPMENT: large disposable foil pan, instant-read thermometer

SERVES: 6

MARINADE

- 2 dried ancho chiles, stems and seeds removed
- ⅓ cup red wine vinegar
- ⅓ cup fresh lemon juice
- ⅓ cup extra-virgin olive oil
- 1 tablespoon ground cumin
- 1 tablespoon dried oregano
- 1 tablespoon kosher salt
- 1 tablespoon finely chopped garlic

- 1 semi-boneless leg of lamb, about 5 pounds

SALSA

- 4 plum tomatoes, about 1 pound total, cut into ¼-inch dice
- 1 English cucumber, about 10 ounces, cut into ¼-inch dice
  Kosher salt
- 3 ounces crumbled feta cheese
- 2 tablespoons red wine vinegar
- 2 tablespoons chopped fresh cilantro leaves
- ½ teaspoon minced garlic
  Ground black pepper

- 4 large handfuls mesquite wood chips, soaked in water for at least 30 minutes

1 In a medium, heavy skillet over medium-high heat, toast the chiles until they are lightly charred, pliable, and dark brick red in spots, 2 to 3 minutes, turning occasionally. Transfer to a plate and let cool. Put the chiles in a food processor or blender and pulse until you have a coarse powder. Pour the powder into a medium bowl and whisk with the remaining marinade ingredients.

2 Place the lamb in a large, resealable plastic bag and pour in the marinade. Press the air out of the bag and seal tightly. Turn the bag to distribute the marinade, place in a large bowl, and refrigerate for 12 to 24 hours, turning the bag occasionally.

3 In a colander toss the tomatoes and cucumber with 1 teaspoon salt and let drain for 1 hour. In a medium bowl combine the tomatoes and cucumber with the remaining salsa ingredients and season with salt and pepper. Cover and refrigerate until ready to serve.

4 Remove the lamb from the bag and discard the marinade. Allow the lamb to stand at room temperature for 30 minutes before cooking.

5 Prepare a two-zone fire for medium heat (350° to 450°F) (see pages 18–19). Place a large disposable foil pan beside the bed of charcoal and fill three-quarters of the way full with water.

6 Brush the cooking grate clean. Drain and add two handfuls of the wood chips to the charcoal and put the lid on the grill. When the wood begins to smoke, cook the lamb over INDIRECT MEDIUM HEAT, with the lid closed, for 45 minutes. Turn the lamb over; drain and add the remaining wood chips to the charcoal. Continue cooking, with the lid closed, until the lamb reaches an internal temperature of 130°F, 40 to 50 minutes for medium rare. Remove from the grill and let rest for 10 to 15 minutes (the internal temperature will rise 5 to 10 degrees during this time).

7 Cut the lamb across the grain into ½-inch slices. Serve warm with the salsa.

A semi-boneless leg of lamb has had the hip bone and the shank removed, which makes for easier cutting.

SMOKED RACKS OF LAMB

WITH BELL PEPPER AND EGGPLANT AJVAR

IDEAL
GRILL:

SMOKE INTENSITY: moderate

PREP TIME: 20 minutes

COOKING TIME: about 40 minutes

SERVES: 4

AJVAR

- 1 globe eggplant, about 1¼ pounds
- 1 red bell pepper, about 8 ounces
- 1 garlic clove
- 2 tablespoons fresh lemon juice
- 1 tablespoon chopped fresh Italian parsley leaves
- ⅓ cup extra-virgin olive oil
  Kosher salt
  Ground black pepper

RUB

- 1 teaspoon cumin seed
- 1 teaspoon coriander seed, lightly crushed
- 1 teaspoon dried oregano
- 1 teaspoon kosher salt
- ½ teaspoon paprika
- ½ teaspoon granulated garlic
- ½ teaspoon ground black pepper
- ½ teaspoon crushed red pepper flakes

- 2 lamb racks, each 1 to 1½ pounds, frenched and trimmed of excess fat
- 1 tablespoon extra-virgin olive oil

- 2 large handfuls oak wood chips, soaked in water for at least 30 minutes

To "french" means to remove the fat from the bones extending from a lamb (or pork) rack or chop, then clean them thoroughly for a nice presentation. Many supermarkets sell racks of lamb with the bones already frenched.

1 Pierce the eggplant several times with a fork. Cut off the top and bottom of the bell pepper. Then make one cut down the side and open it up into a large strip. Cut away the ribs and seeds.

2 Prepare a two-zone fire for medium heat (350° to 450°F) (see pages 18–19).

3 Brush the cooking grate clean. Cook the eggplant over DIRECT MEDIUM HEAT, with the lid closed as much as possible, until soft and beginning to collapse, about 20 minutes, turning occasionally. At the same time, cook the bell pepper, shiny skin side down, over DIRECT MEDIUM HEAT, until the skin is blackened and blistered, 8 to 10 minutes (do not turn). Remove from the grill as they are done. Put the bell pepper in a small bowl and cover with plastic wrap to trap the steam. Let stand for about 10 minutes. Remove from the bowl and peel away and discard the charred skin. Cut the eggplant in half lengthwise and scoop out the pulp. Discard the skin and any large seed pockets.

4 In a food processor whirl the garlic until it is minced. Add the eggplant pulp, bell pepper, lemon juice, and parsley and pulse to create a thick sauce. With the machine running, slowly add the oil and process until the *ajvar* is smooth and emulsified. Season with salt and pepper.

5 In a small bowl combine the rub ingredients. Lightly brush the lamb with the oil and season evenly with the rub. Allow the lamb to stand at room temperature for 15 to 30 minutes before cooking.

6 Replenish the charcoal if needed to maintain a steady temperature, adding 6 to 10 lit briquettes after 45 minutes.

7 Drain and add the wood chips to the charcoal and put the lid on the grill. When the wood begins to smoke, cook the lamb, bone side down first, over DIRECT MEDIUM HEAT, with the lid closed as much as possible, for 5 minutes, turning once (watch for flare-ups). Move the lamb over INDIRECT MEDIUM HEAT and continue cooking to your desired doneness, about 15 minutes more for medium rare, turning once or twice. Remove from the grill and let rest for 3 to 5 minutes. Cut the lamb racks between the bones into individual chops. Serve warm with the *ajvar*.

RED MEAT

BEER-BRAISED AND MESQUITE-SMOKED SHORT RIBS

IDEAL
GRILL:

SMOKE INTENSITY: moderate

PREP TIME: 45 minutes

BRAISING TIME: about 1½ hours

CHILLING TIME: about 2 hours

REDUCING TIME: 1 to 1½ hours

COOKING TIME: about 30 minutes

SPECIAL EQUIPMENT: large stockpot

SERVES: 4

BRAISING LIQUID
- 1 tablespoon extra-virgin olive oil
- 1 yellow onion, about 10 ounces, roughly chopped
- 6 garlic cloves, roughly chopped
- 1 jalapeño chile pepper, about 1 ounce, roughly chopped (with seeds)
- 2 teaspoons dried oregano
- 2 teaspoons cumin seed
- 1 teaspoon kosher salt
- ½ teaspoon ground black pepper
- 3 bottles (each 12 fluid ounces) lager
- 1 bay leaf

- 5 pounds meaty beef short ribs

SAUCE
- 1 cup ketchup
- 2 tablespoons molasses
- 1 tablespoon balsamic vinegar
- 2 teaspoons Worcestershire sauce
  Hot pepper sauce (optional)

- 2 tablespoons extra-virgin olive oil
- 1 teaspoon kosher salt
- ½ teaspoon ground black pepper

- 2 large handfuls mesquite wood chips, soaked in water for at least 30 minutes

Look for individually cut short ribs (sometimes called English-style ribs) for this recipe. Pass over flanken-style (crosscut) ribs and boneless short ribs.

1 In a large stockpot over medium heat, heat the oil. Add the onion, garlic, and jalapeño and cook until the onion is tender, about 5 minutes, stirring occasionally. Add the oregano, cumin seed, salt, and pepper and cook until fragrant, about 30 seconds, stirring constantly. Pour in the lager and add the bay leaf. Place the ribs in the braising liquid, meaty side down, and add just enough water to cover them. Bring to a boil over high heat and then reduce the heat to low. Cover and simmer until the ribs are barely tender when pierced with the tip of a knife, about 1½ hours. Transfer the ribs to a sheet pan to cool. Remove and discard any bones that may have fallen off the ribs in the liquid; reserve the liquid. Cover and refrigerate the cooled ribs until chilled, about 2 hours.

2 Strain the braising liquid through a fine mesh strainer into a large bowl and let stand for 10 minutes. Skim the fat from the surface of the liquid. Rinse the stockpot, pour the liquid back into the stockpot, and bring to a boil over high heat. Lower the heat and simmer the liquid until reduced to ¾ cup, 1 to 1½ hours. Transfer to a medium saucepan. Stir in the ketchup, molasses, balsamic vinegar, and Worcestershire sauce. Bring to a simmer over medium heat, then reduce the heat to low, and simmer until the sauce is slightly reduced, about 5 minutes, stirring often. Remove from the heat and season with hot pepper sauce, if desired. Set aside at room temperature.

3 Prepare a two-zone fire for medium heat (350° to 450°F) (see pages 18–19).

4 Brush the ribs with the oil and season evenly with the salt and pepper. Brush the cooking grate clean. Drain and add one handful of the wood chips to the charcoal and put the lid on the grill. When the wood begins to smoke, cook the ribs over INDIRECT MEDIUM HEAT, with the lid closed, until the meat begins to crisp around the edges and the ribs are heated through, about 25 minutes.

5 Brush the ribs generously with the sauce. Drain and add the remaining wood chips to the charcoal. Move the ribs over DIRECT MEDIUM HEAT, close the lid, and continue to cook until the meat is glazed, about 5 minutes, turning occasionally. Remove from the grill and serve warm with the remaining sauce.

Be sure the ribs are chilled before cooking them so they have a longer reheating period and can soak up more smoke flavor.

BIG BEEF BACK RIBS
WITH PLUM-RUM BARBECUE SAUCE

IDEAL
GRILL:

SMOKE INTENSITY: strong

PREP TIME: 40 minutes

COOKING TIME: about 4 hours

SERVES: 6

RUB

 2 tablespoons paprika
 2 tablespoons packed dark brown sugar,
   preferably *muscovado*
 2 teaspoons ground cinnamon
 2 teaspoons dried thyme
 2 teaspoons kosher salt
 2 teaspoons ground black pepper
 1 teaspoon grated nutmeg
 ½ teaspoon ground allspice
 ½ teaspoon ground mace

 2 racks beef back ribs, each about
   4 pounds
 ¼ cup Worcestershire sauce

 8 large hickory wood chunks

SAUCE

 4 large, ripe black plums, about
   1¼ pounds total, chopped
 1⅓ cups canned crushed tomatoes
 ¼ cup minced shallots (1 ounce)
 ¼ cup granulated sugar
 ¼ cup dark rum
 ¼ cup Grade B maple syrup
 ¼ cup cider vinegar
 2 tablespoons Dijon mustard
 2 tablespoons Worcestershire sauce
 2 tablespoons peeled, minced
   fresh ginger
 ½ teaspoon ground black pepper
 ¼ teaspoon ground cloves

Beef back ribs are cut from a rib roast. Don't confuse them with short ribs, which are bigger with much tougher meat.

1 In a small bowl mix the rub ingredients.

2 Use a dull dinner knife to help peel the translucent, papery membrane off the back of the racks. Cut each rack in half to make four slabs. Rub the Worcestershire sauce onto the slabs and then pat and smear the rub all over them. Set aside at room temperature while you prepare the smoker.

3 Prepare the smoker for indirect cooking with very low heat (200° to 250°F) (see pages 20–21). When the temperature reaches 225°F, add two hickory wood chunks to the charcoal.

4 Brush the cooking grate clean. Smoke the slabs, bone side down, over INDIRECT VERY LOW HEAT, with the lid closed, until they are just tender, about 3½ hours. Add more lit briquettes as necessary to maintain a steady, even heat between 200° and 250°F, and add two more wood chunks to the charcoal every 45 minutes. Meanwhile, make the sauce.

5 In a large, heavy-bottomed saucepan whisk the sauce ingredients. Bring to a boil over medium-high heat, stirring occasionally. Reduce the heat to medium-low and simmer, uncovered, until the plums are very soft and the sauce has lightly thickened, about 20 minutes, stirring often. Remove from the heat and puree in a blender, food processor, or with an immersion blender until smooth.

6 After the slabs have been in the smoker for 3½ hours (they will look quite dark), baste their tops with some of the sauce and continue smoking over INDIRECT VERY LOW HEAT, with the lid closed, for about 15 minutes. Turn the slabs over, baste with more sauce, and cook until the slabs are glazed and tender, about 15 minutes more. Remove from the smoker and let rest for about 10 minutes. Cut between the bones and serve the ribs warm with the remaining sauce.

To tell if the beef ribs are tender, insert a meat fork into the meat between the bones. It should go in very easily.

PEPPER-CRUSTED RIB ROAST

WITH THREE-HERB HAZELNUT PESTO

IDEAL GRILL:

SMOKE INTENSITY: moderate

PREP TIME: 30 minutes

COOKING TIME: about 2¼ hours

SPECIAL EQUIPMENT:
instant-read thermometer

SERVES: 6 to 8

2　tablespoons coarsely crushed
　black peppercorns
1　tablespoon kosher salt
1　three-bone beef roast,
　about 7¼ pounds
1　tablespoon canola oil

PESTO
½　cup loosely packed fresh
　cilantro leaves
½　cup loosely packed fresh Italian
　parsley leaves
¼　cup loosely packed fresh
　oregano leaves
¼　cup hazelnuts, toasted and
　skins removed
¼　cup sherry vinegar
3–5　medium garlic cloves,
　roughly chopped
½　teaspoon crushed red pepper flakes
½　cup extra-virgin olive oil

　Kosher salt
　Ground black pepper

2　large handfuls apple or oak wood
　chips, soaked in water for at least
　30 minutes

1　In a small bowl mix the peppercorns and salt. Coat the roast on all sides with the oil and season evenly with the peppercorn mixture. Allow the roast to stand at room temperature for 1 hour before grilling.

2　In a food processor or blender process the pesto ingredients, except the oil. Then, with the motor running, slowly add the oil to make a thin paste. Season with salt and pepper. Pour into a serving bowl, cover, and let stand at room temperature while cooking the roast.

3　Prepare the grill for indirect cooking over medium-low heat (about 350°F) (see pages 22–23).

4　Brush the cooking grates clean. Drain and add one handful of the wood chips to the smoker box of a gas grill, following manufacturer's instructions, and close the lid. When smoke appears, cook the roast, bone side down, over **INDIRECT MEDIUM-LOW HEAT**, with the lid closed, until the internal temperature reaches 120° to 125°F for medium rare, about 2¼ hours. Drain and add the remaining wood chips to the smoker box after the first hour of cooking.

5　Remove the roast from the grill and let rest for about 20 minutes (the internal temperature will rise 5 to 10 degrees during this time). Cut the roast into thick slices and serve warm with the pesto.

To toast and skin the hazelnuts, spread the nuts on a rimmed baking sheet. Bake in a preheated 350°F oven until the skins are cracked, about 10 minutes, stirring occasionally. Transfer to a clean kitchen towel and let cool for 10 minutes. Wrap and rub the cooled nuts in the towel to remove the skins (some skin will remain).

Pork

BRINED AND MAPLE-SMOKED BACON

IDEAL GRILL:

SMOKE INTENSITY: strong

PREP TIME: 15 minutes

BRINING TIME: 48 hours

REFRIGERATION TIME: 12 hours

COOKING TIME: about 3 hours

SPECIAL EQUIPMENT:
instant-read thermometer

SERVES: 12

BRINE

- 3½ quarts water
- 1 cup kosher salt
- 1 cup honey
- 1 cup maple syrup, preferably Grade B
- 1½ teaspoons pink curing salt

- 2 pieces pork belly, about 4 pounds total, rind removed
- 1 tablespoon black peppercorns, coarsely crushed

- 9 maple wood chunks

1 In a large, nonreactive pot whisk the brine ingredients until the salt is dissolved. Add the pork bellies and top with a plate to keep them submerged. Cover and refrigerate for 48 hours, no longer.

2 Remove the pork bellies from the pot and discard the brine. Rinse the pork under cold running water and pat dry with paper towels. Spread the crushed peppercorns on a cutting board and press into the long side of each piece of pork belly. Set the pork bellies on a large wire rack set over a large sheet pan. Refrigerate, uncovered, for 12 hours.

3 Prepare the smoker for indirect cooking with very low heat (200° to 250°F) (see pages 20–21). When the temperature reaches 225°F, add three of the wood chunks to the charcoal.

4 Brush the cooking grate clean. Smoke the pork bellies over **INDIRECT VERY LOW HEAT**, with the lid closed, until an instant-read thermometer inserted into each piece registers 150°F, about 3 hours. Add more lit briquettes as necessary to maintain the heat and add three more wood chunks to the charcoal after the first and second hours. Remove from the smoker and cool completely.

5 Remove any stray bones before using. The bacon can be wrapped in plastic wrap and refrigerated for up to 1 week. Or wrap the bacon in plastic and then wrap again in aluminum foil and freeze for up to 3 months.

If you slice your home-smoked bacon by hand, without a delicatessen-style machine, the slices will be on the thick side (see photo at left), so plan on a little extra time when pan-frying them. Or you can simply cut the bacon into chunks for flavoring soups and stews.

TERIYAKI PORK BELLY
WITH CASHEW JASMINE RICE

IDEAL GRILL:

SMOKE INTENSITY: moderate

PREP TIME: 30 minutes

BRAISING TIME: about 3 hours

CHILLING TIME: about 2 hours

REDUCING TIME: 1 to 1¼ hours

COOKING TIME: about 1½ hours

SPECIAL EQUIPMENT: 5-quart Dutch oven, instant-read thermometer

SERVES: 6

BRAISING LIQUID

- 1 quart water
- ¾ cup roughly chopped scallions (white and light green parts only)
- ½ cup soy sauce
- ⅓ cup bourbon
- ⅓ cup packed light brown sugar
- 2 ounces fresh ginger, peeled and cut into ½-inch slices
- 3 tablespoons hoisin sauce
- 2 whole star anise
- 2 garlic cloves, peeled and crushed

- 1 pork belly (with rind), about 2½ pounds

- 4 fist-sized apple or cherry wood chunks

RICE

- 1½ cups jasmine rice
- 2¼ cups water
- ¾ teaspoon kosher salt
- ½ cup coarsely chopped roasted cashews
- ⅓ cup thinly sliced scallions (white and light green parts only)

Pork belly can be purchased at Asian butcher shops and some supermarkets. It is the same cut of pork used for bacon. There are three components to a pork belly, arranged in layers: rind, fat, and meat. Choose a pork belly with a good proportion of pink meat compared to the white fat. Like bacon, some of the fat will remain intact when serving the pork belly, so don't expect it to melt away during braising.

1 In a 5-quart Dutch oven over high heat, combine the braising liquid ingredients and bring to a simmer, stirring constantly to dissolve the sugar. Place the pork belly in the braising liquid, rind side down, and add more water if needed to barely cover it. Bring to a boil over high heat and then reduce the heat to low. Cover and simmer until the pork is very tender when pierced with the tip of a sharp knife, about 3 hours, turning occasionally and adding more water as needed to keep the pork covered. Transfer the pork to a platter to cool. Reserve the liquid to make the sauce. Cover the pork with plastic wrap and refrigerate until chilled, about 2 hours.

2 Set a fine mesh strainer over a large bowl and strain the braising liquid. Discard the solids that remain in the strainer. Let stand for 10 minutes. Skim the fat from the surface of the liquid. Rinse the Dutch oven, pour the liquid back into the pot, and bring to a boil over high heat. Lower the heat and simmer the liquid until reduced to 1 cup, 1 to 1¼ hours. Let cool. Cover and refrigerate until ready to use.

3 Prepare the smoker for indirect cooking with very low heat (200° to 250°F) (see pages 20–21). When the temperature reaches 225°F, add three of the wood chunks to the charcoal.

4 Brush the cooking grate clean. Smoke the pork belly, rind side up, over **INDIRECT VERY LOW HEAT**, with the lid closed, for 1 hour. Then add the remaining wood chunk to the charcoal and continue to smoke the pork until the internal temperature reaches 140°F, about 30 minutes more. Transfer to a cutting board and let rest for about 10 minutes (the internal temperature will rise 5 to 10 degrees during this time).

5 About 25 minutes before the pork is done, make the rice. Put the rice in a fine mesh strainer and rinse well under cold running water; drain. In a medium saucepan over high heat, bring the rice, water, and salt to a boil. Reduce the heat to medium-low. Cover and simmer until the rice is tender and has absorbed the water, 17 to 20 minutes. Remove from the heat and add the cashews and scallions, but do not stir. Cover the saucepan again and let stand for 5 to 10 minutes. Fold in the cashews and scallions and fluff the rice.

6 Reheat the sauce. Cut the pork crosswise into ½-inch slices. Spoon the rice into serving bowls, top with slices of pork, and drizzle generously with the sauce. Serve warm with any remaining sauce.

CANADIAN BACON WITH APPLE WOOD SMOKE

IDEAL GRILL:

SMOKE INTENSITY: strong

PREP TIME: 30 minutes

BRINING TIME: 48 hours

REFRIGERATION TIME: 12 hours

COOKING TIME: 1¾ to 2 hours

SPECIAL EQUIPMENT: butcher's twine, instant-read thermometer

SERVES: 16

BRINE

¼ cup juniper berries
2 quarts water
1 quart unsweetened apple cider
1 quart lager
1 cup kosher salt
1 cup packed dark brown sugar, preferably *muscovado*
1 cup loosely packed fresh sage leaves
1 cup loosely packed, roughly chopped fresh thyme sprigs
2 tablespoons pink curing salt
1 tablespoon black peppercorns
4 medium garlic cloves, crushed

1 boneless, center-cut pork loin roast, about 4 pounds, trimmed of excess fat
  Vegetable oil
4 apple wood chunks

1 Crush the juniper berries under a heavy pot. Transfer them to a very large, nonreactive bowl and mix in the remaining brine ingredients, stirring constantly to dissolve the salt and sugar.

2 Cut the roast in half lengthwise, and then tie each half with butcher's twine at 2-inch intervals to make a compact cylinder. Add the roasts to the brine and then place a plate on top to keep them submerged. Cover and refrigerate for 48 hours.

3 Remove the roasts from the bowl, and discard the brine. Set the roasts on a wire rack on a sheet pan. Refrigerate, uncovered, for 12 hours. The surface of the meat will appear dry. Allow the roasts to stand at room temperature for 15 to 30 minutes before cooking. Brush the roasts all over with oil.

4 Prepare the smoker for indirect cooking with very low heat (200° to 250°F) (see pages 20–21). When the temperature reaches 225°F, add two wood chunks to the charcoal.

5 Brush the cooking grate clean. Smoke the roasts, fat side up, over **INDIRECT VERY LOW HEAT**, with the lid closed, for 1 hour, adjusting the vents so the temperature inside the smoker stays as close to 225°F as possible.

6 Add the remaining wood chunks to the charcoal. Continue smoking over **INDIRECT VERY LOW HEAT**, with the lid closed, until an instant-read thermometer inserted into the center of each roast registers 150°F, 45 minutes to 1 hour. Remove from the smoker and let rest for about 10 minutes. Remove the twine and cut the meat crosswise into thin slices. Serve warm.

Pink curing salt (see photo at left) is also called sodium nitrate, usually tinted pink so it isn't confused with regular salt. Pink curing salt is used in charcuterie to discourage bacterial growth and to give the meat an appetizing color. Do not confuse it with Himalayan and Hawaiian pink salts, which are naturally pink and are considered finishing salts.

CEDAR-PLANKED PORK TENDERLOINS
WITH MANGO AND CURRY

IDEAL GRILL:

SMOKE INTENSITY: moderate

PREP TIME: 20 minutes

COOKING TIME: 25 to 30 minutes

SPECIAL EQUIPMENT: 1 untreated cedar plank, 12 to 15 inches long and about 7 inches wide and ½ to ¾ inch thick, soaked in water for at least 1 hour; instant-read thermometer

SERVES: 6

Whenever you are cooking with a plank, keep it over direct heat as long as possible to generate a good amount of smoke, but if you see flames coming from the plank at any time, move it over indirect heat.

RUB
- 2 teaspoons curry powder
- 1 teaspoon dried thyme
- 1 teaspoon kosher salt
- ½ teaspoon ground black pepper

- 2 pork tenderloins, each about 1 pound, trimmed of excess fat and silver skin
  Vegetable or canola oil

SAUCE
- 2 ripe mangoes, about 1½ pounds total, roughly chopped
- 2 tablespoons fresh lime juice
- ¼ teaspoon curry powder
- ¼ teaspoon toasted sesame oil
- ¼ teaspoon kosher salt
- ¼ teaspoon hot pepper sauce

- 1 tablespoon finely chopped fresh cilantro leaves (optional)

1 In a small bowl mix the rub ingredients. Lightly coat the pork tenderloins on all sides with oil and season evenly with the rub. Allow the tenderloins to stand at room temperature for 15 to 30 minutes before grilling.

2 Prepare the grill for direct and indirect cooking over medium-high heat (400° to 450°F) (see pages 22–23).

3 In a food processor or blender puree the sauce ingredients. If the sauce is too thick, thin with water 1 tablespoon at a time. You should have about ⅔ cup of sauce.

4 Brush the cooking grates clean. Place the soaked plank over DIRECT MEDIUM-HIGH HEAT and close the lid. After 5 to 10 minutes, when the plank begins to smoke and char, turn the plank over. Arrange the tenderloins on the plank and cook over DIRECT MEDIUM-HIGH HEAT, with the lid closed, for 10 minutes. Then move the plank over INDIRECT MEDIUM-HIGH HEAT and continue cooking, with the lid closed, until the internal temperature reaches 145°F, 15 to 20 minutes, turning the tenderloins once. Remove from the grill and let rest for 3 to 5 minutes.

5 Cut the tenderloins crosswise into thick slices, top with the cilantro, if desired, and serve with the mango sauce.

HICKORY PORK TENDERLOINS
WITH CITRUS-CILANTRO SAUCE

IDEAL GRILL:

SMOKE INTENSITY: moderate

PREP TIME: 20 minutes

COOKING TIME: about 18 minutes

SPECIAL EQUIPMENT:
instant-read thermometer

SERVES: 4

Add the food to the grill when the coals reach about 375°F, the lower half of the medium temperature range. This will allow the pork to be in contact with the smoke for a longer period of time and soak up more smoke flavor. It will also keep the glaze from scorching, which is a possibility at higher temperatures.

SAUCE

  2 navel oranges
  1 lime
  ½ cup granulated sugar
  ½ cup bourbon
  ½ cup finely chopped fresh
     cilantro leaves

  2 pork tenderloins, each ¾ to 1 pound,
     trimmed of excess fat and silver skin
     Extra-virgin olive oil
  1 teaspoon kosher salt
  ½ teaspoon crushed red pepper flakes

  1 large handful hickory wood chips,
     soaked in water for at least 30 minutes

1 Finely grate the zest from the oranges and lime and set aside. Juice the oranges (you should have ⅔ cup juice) and the lime (you should have 3 tablespoons juice). In a medium, heavy-bottomed saucepan over medium-high heat, combine the orange and lime juice and the sugar and bring to a boil, stirring just until the sugar is dissolved. Continue cooking, without stirring, until the mixture is covered with large, glossy bubbles and is reduced to about ½ cup. Remove from the heat. Carefully stir in the bourbon, taking care that it doesn't ignite. Return the saucepan over medium-high heat and bring to a boil. Cook until syrupy and reduced again to ½ cup, stirring occasionally. Pour into a heatproof container and let cool completely. Stir in the orange and lime zest and the cilantro.

2 Lightly brush the tenderloins with oil and season evenly with the salt and red pepper flakes.

3 Prepare a two-zone fire for medium heat (350° to 450°F) (see pages 18–19).

4 Brush the cooking grate clean. Drain and add the wood chips to the charcoal and put the lid on the grill. When the wood begins to smoke, cook the tenderloins over DIRECT MEDIUM HEAT, with the lid closed as much as possible, until the outsides are seared and golden brown, about 10 minutes, turning occasionally. Then generously brush the tops with some of the sauce, close the lid, and cook for 3 minutes. Turn the pork over and brush with more sauce. Close the lid, and cook until the internal temperature reaches 145°F, about 5 minutes more. Remove from the grill and let rest for 3 to 5 minutes. Cut the tenderloins crosswise into ½-inch slices and serve with the remaining sauce.

WOOD-SMOKED PORK TACOS
WITH BLACK BEAN SALSA

IDEAL GRILL:

SMOKE INTENSITY: mild

PREP TIME: 30 minutes

COOKING TIME: 30 to 35 minutes

SPECIAL EQUIPMENT: instant-read thermometer, large disposable foil pan

SERVES: 4 to 6

Don't be tempted to cook the pork directly over the coals. Slower cooking ensures a smokier flavor.

SALSA
- 1 can (15 ounces) black beans, rinsed
- 1 cup finely chopped tomato
- ½ cup finely chopped tomatillos
- 2 tablespoons finely chopped fresh cilantro leaves
- 2 tablespoons extra-virgin olive oil
- 1 tablespoon fresh lime juice
- 1 tablespoon minced serrano chile pepper
- 1 teaspoon minced garlic

  Kosher salt
  Ground black pepper

RUB
- ½ teaspoon prepared chili powder
- ½ teaspoon ground cumin
- ¼ teaspoon granulated garlic

- 1 pork tenderloin, about 1 pound, trimmed of excess fat and silver skin
  Extra-virgin olive oil
- 2 large handfuls mesquite wood chips, soaked in water for at least 30 minutes
- 12 corn tortillas (6 inches)
  Store-bought guacamole

1 In a medium, nonreactive bowl combine the salsa ingredients. Season with salt and pepper. Mix gently but thoroughly. If desired, to fully incorporate the flavors, let the salsa sit at room temperature for up to 1 hour.

2 Prepare a two-zone fire for high heat (450° to 550°F) (see pages 18–19).

3 In a small bowl mix the rub ingredients, including ½ teaspoon salt and ¼ teaspoon pepper. Lightly brush the tenderloin all over with oil and season evenly with the rub. Set aside at room temperature for 15 to 30 minutes before cooking.

4 Brush the cooking grate clean. Drain and add the wood chips to the charcoal and put the lid on the grill. When the wood begins to smoke, cook the tenderloin over INDIRECT HIGH HEAT, with the lid closed as much as possible, until the internal temperature reaches 145°F, 20 to 25 minutes. Remove from the grill and wrap with aluminum foil. Let rest for about 15 minutes or until cool enough to handle.

5 Cut the tenderloin crosswise into six pieces. Shred the meat and transfer to a large disposable foil pan. Add the salsa and mix well. About 15 minutes before you are ready to serve, warm the pork and black bean salsa over INDIRECT LOW OR MEDIUM HEAT for about 10 minutes. Meanwhile, brush one side of each tortilla with oil and lightly season with salt. Grill the tortillas, oil side down, over direct heat for about 1 minute (do not turn). Divide the pork and salsa among the tortillas and serve with guacamole.

CHILE-RUBBED PORK CHOPS
WITH SMOKED TOMATILLO SAUCE

IDEAL
GRILL:

SMOKE INTENSITY: moderate

PREP TIME: 25 minutes

MARINATING TIME: 20 to 30 minutes

COOKING TIME: 8 to 10 minutes

SPECIAL EQUIPMENT:
perforated grill pan

SERVES: 4

RUB

2 teaspoons pure chile powder
2 teaspoons garlic powder
1 teaspoon ground cumin

   Kosher salt
   Ground black pepper

4 bone-in pork loin chops, each about
   8 ounces and 1 inch thick, trimmed of
   excess fat
   Extra-virgin olive oil

4 tomatillos, about 9 ounces total,
   papery husks removed, rinsed, each
   cut in half
2 slices white onion, each about
   ¼ inch thick
1 large jalapeño chile pepper,
   about 1½ ounces, halved lengthwise,
   seeds removed

2 large handfuls mesquite wood chips,
   soaked in water for at least 30 minutes

½ cup loosely packed fresh cilantro
   leaves, roughly chopped
½ teaspoon packed light brown sugar

A jalapeño chile pepper gives the sauce a kick, and removing the seeds makes it milder. For extra zip, add the seeds or toss in another jalapeño.

1 In a small bowl mix the rub ingredients, including 1 teaspoon salt and ½ teaspoon pepper. Lightly brush the pork chops on both sides with oil and season evenly with the rub. Cover and marinate at room temperature for 20 to 30 minutes.

2 Prepare a two-zone fire for medium heat (350° to 450°F) (see pages 18–19) and preheat the grill pan on the cooking grate.

3 Lightly brush the tomatillos, onion, and jalapeño with oil.

4 Brush the cooking grate clean. Drain and add the wood chips to the charcoal and put the lid on the grill. When the wood begins to smoke, arrange the vegetables in a single layer on the grill pan and place the chops on the cooking grate. Cook over DIRECT MEDIUM HEAT, with the lid closed as much as possible, until the vegetables are crisp-tender and the chops are still slightly pink in the center, 8 to 10 minutes, turning once or twice. Remove the vegetables and chops from the grill and let the chops rest for 3 to 5 minutes.

5 Cut the vegetables into bite-sized pieces and place in a bowl. Add the cilantro and brown sugar and toss to combine. Season with salt and pepper. Serve the pork chops warm with the tomatillo sauce.

BEST-ON-THE-BLOCK BABY BACK RIBS

IDEAL GRILL:

SMOKE INTENSITY: moderate

PREP TIME: 30 minutes

COOKING TIME: about 3 hours

SPECIAL EQUIPMENT:
rib rack, small spray bottle

SERVES: 6 to 8

RUB
- 2 tablespoons kosher salt
- 1 tablespoon smoked paprika
- 1 tablespoon granulated garlic
- 1 tablespoon pure chile powder
- 2 teaspoons mustard powder
- 2 teaspoons dried thyme
- 1 teaspoon ground cumin
- 1 teaspoon celery seed
- 1 teaspoon ground black pepper

- 4 racks baby back ribs, each 2½ to 3 pounds

- 4 large handfuls hickory wood chips, soaked in water for at least 30 minutes

SAUCE
- 4 slices bacon
- 1 cup ketchup
- ½ cup unsweetened apple juice
- ¼ cup cider vinegar
- 1 tablespoon molasses
- 2 teaspoons Worcestershire sauce
- ½ teaspoon smoked paprika
- ½ teaspoon ground cumin
- ¼ teaspoon kosher salt
- ¼ teaspoon ground black pepper
  Hot pepper sauce (optional)

MOP
- ½ cup unsweetened apple juice
- 1 tablespoon cider vinegar

These ribs are their tender best when slow cooked with low indirect heat from all sides. Cooking them on a big, six-burner gas grill (equipped with a smoker box) will allow you to arrange all four racks in the center of the cooking grates, without any of them hanging over the direct heat from the outside burners. If you are using a smaller grill, it would be wise to cook just two or three racks.

1 In a small bowl mix the rub ingredients. Using a dull dinner knife, slide the tip under the membrane covering the back of each rack of ribs. Lift and loosen the membrane until it breaks, then grab a corner of it with a paper towel and pull it off. Season the racks evenly with the rub. Arrange the racks in the rib rack, standing each rack up and facing in the same direction. Let the racks stand at room temperature for 30 minutes to 1 hour before cooking.

2 Prepare the grill for indirect cooking over low heat (300° to 350°F) (see pages 22–23).

3 Brush the cooking grates clean. Drain and add two handfuls of the wood chips to the smoker box of a gas grill, following manufacturer's instructions, and close the lid. When the wood begins to smoke, cook the racks over INDIRECT LOW HEAT, with the lid closed, for 1 hour. Maintain the temperature of the grill between 300° and 350°F.

4 In a medium skillet over low heat, cook the bacon until brown and crispy, 10 to 15 minutes, turning occasionally. Drain the bacon on paper towels and eat the bacon whenever you like, but reserve the bacon fat in the skillet and let it cool to room temperature. In a medium saucepan combine all the remaining sauce ingredients, except the hot pepper sauce. Add 3 tablespoons of the bacon fat, whisk until smooth, and cook over low heat for about 5 minutes. If you like a spicy sauce, season with hot pepper sauce. Remove the saucepan from the heat.

5 In a small spray bottle or bowl combine the mop ingredients. After the first hour of cooking, drain and add the remaining wood chips to the smoker box. Lightly spray or brush the racks with the mop, particularly the areas that are looking a little dry. Close the lid and cook for a second hour. Maintain the temperature of the grill between 300° and 350°F.

6 After the second hour of cooking, lightly spray or brush the racks with the mop, particularly the areas that are looking a little dry. If any racks are cooking faster than the others or look much darker, swap their positions for even cooking. Cook for another 30 minutes or so.

7 After 2½ hours, the meat will shrink back from most of the bones by ¼ inch or more. If it has not, continue to cook until it does. Then remove the racks in the rib rack from the grill. Close the lid of the grill to maintain the heat. Remove the racks from the rib rack and lightly brush each rack on both sides with some of the sauce.

8 Return the racks to the grill over INDIRECT LOW HEAT. At this point you can pile all the racks on top of one another or stack the racks two to a pile. Continue to cook over INDIRECT LOW HEAT, with the lid closed, until tender and succulent, 15 to 30 minutes. They are done when you lift a rack at one end with tongs, bone side up, and the rack bends so much in the middle that the meat tears easily. If the meat does not tear easily, continue to cook until it does. Just before serving, lightly brush the racks with sauce again. Cut the racks into individual ribs and serve warm.

PACIFIC RIM PORK ROAST
WITH MANGO SALSA

IDEAL GRILL:

SMOKE INTENSITY: strong

PREP TIME: 30 minutes

COOKING TIME: 8 to 10 hours

SPECIAL EQUIPMENT:
spice mill, instant-read thermometer

SERVES: 8 to 10

1 bone-in pork shoulder roast
(Boston butt), 7 to 8 pounds
5 teaspoons Hawaiian red salt
2 teaspoons Sichuan peppercorns
1 teaspoon black peppercorns

MOP
¾ cup pineapple juice, preferably
refrigerated instead of canned
2 tablespoons whole-grain mustard
2 tablespoons cider vinegar

4 fist-sized apple wood chunks

SALSA
4 mangoes, about 2 pounds total,
cut into ¼-inch dice
2 scallions (white and light green
parts only), finely chopped
3 tablespoons fresh lime juice
2 tablespoons finely chopped fresh
Thai basil or mint leaves
1 tablespoon Thai fish sauce
1 tablespoon peeled, minced
fresh ginger
1 small Thai or serrano chile
pepper, seeded and minced (about
½ teaspoon)

2 heads Boston lettuce or other leafy
green lettuce, separated into leaves

1 Using a very sharp knife, trim the roast's exterior fat so that it is no thicker than ¼ inch. In a spice mill whirl the salt and the peppercorns until finely ground. Rub the mixture all over the roast and let stand at room temperature for 1 hour before grilling.

2 In a small, nonreactive bowl whisk the mop ingredients and set aside.

3 Prepare the smoker for indirect cooking with very low heat (200° to 250°F) (see pages 20–21). When the temperature reaches 225°F, add two wood chunks to the charcoal.

4 Brush the cooking grate clean. Smoke the roast, fat side up, over INDIRECT VERY LOW HEAT, with the lid closed, until the internal temperature registers 190°F, 8 to 10 hours, turning once after 4 hours. Add one more wood chunk after the first and second hours and brush both sides of the roast with the mop every hour. Maintain the temperature of the smoker between 225° to 250°F by adjusting the vents and adding more lit briquettes as necessary. Transfer the roast to a platter, loosely cover with foil, and let rest for about 30 minutes. Meanwhile, make the salsa.

5 In a large, nonreactive bowl mix the salsa ingredients. Cover and refrigerate until serving.

6 Using two forks or your fingers, pull the pork apart into shreds, discarding any pockets of fat. Pile the pulled pork onto individual lettuce leaves and top with the mango salsa. Serve warm or at room temperature.

Hawaiian red salt has a complex mineral flavor and is available at specialty food stores and online.

QUINTESSENTIAL PULLED PORK SANDWICHES

IDEAL
GRILL:

SMOKE INTENSITY: strong

PREP TIME: 30 minutes

COOKING TIME: 8 to 10 hours

RESTING TIME: 1 hour

SPECIAL EQUIPMENT: food syringe,
instant-read thermometer

SERVES: 12

1   bone-in pork shoulder roast (Boston
    butt), 7 to 8 pounds

½   cup unsweetened apple juice
    Kosher salt
1   tablespoon packed light brown sugar
1   tablespoon Worcestershire sauce

RUB

1   tablespoon packed light brown sugar
2   teaspoons paprika
1   teaspoon prepared chili powder
1   teaspoon granulated garlic
1   teaspoon mustard powder
1   teaspoon ground black pepper

10 fist-sized hickory wood chunks

SAUCE

1½ cups ketchup
¾   cup unsweetened apple juice
¾   cup cider vinegar
3   tablespoons packed light brown sugar
3   tablespoons tomato paste
1½ tablespoons molasses
1   tablespoon Worcestershire sauce
1½ teaspoons mustard powder
¾   teaspoon hot pepper sauce
½   teaspoon ground black pepper

12 hamburger buns
4   cups purchased or homemade coleslaw

Patience. A pork shoulder can be a tough, ornery cut of meat. It takes time to break down the muscle fibers and to melt the connective tissues. So get yourself a reliable thermometer and wait as long as it takes for your pork shoulder to reach 190°F before you try to pull or shred the meat. This recipe is worth every minute it requires.

1   Using a very sharp knife, trim the roast's exterior fat so that it is no thicker than ¼ inch. In a small bowl whisk the apple juice, 2 tablespoons salt, brown sugar, Worcestershire sauce, and ¼ cup water until the salt and sugar have dissolved. Then inject the roast with the liquid flavoring: With the fat side facing down, imagine the roast in 1-inch squares and, using a food syringe, inject each square with some of the liquid, slowly pulling the needle out as you inject the liquid. Some liquid will seep out, but try to keep as much as possible inside the roast.

2   In a small bowl mix the rub ingredients including 2 teaspoons salt. Coat the surface of the roast evenly with the rub. Allow the roast to stand at room temperature for 30 minutes before cooking.

3   Prepare the smoker for indirect cooking with very low heat (200° to 250°F) (see pages 20–21). When the temperature reaches 225°F, add two wood chunks to the charcoal.

4   Brush the cooking grate clean. Smoke the roast, fat side up, over INDIRECT VERY LOW HEAT, with the lid closed, for 5 hours, adjusting the vents so the temperature of the smoker stays as close to 225°F as possible. At the start of every hour (after the first hour), add two more wood chunks to the charcoal. If the temperature falls below 200°F and can't be raised by adjusting the vents, add more lit briquettes as needed.

5   After 5 hours, use an instant-read thermometer to check the internal temperature of the meat. If it has not reached 160°F, continue cooking until it does. If it has reached 160°F, remove the meat from the smoker. Put the lid back on the smoker to prevent heat loss. Add more lit briquettes and refill the water pan to maintain the 225°F temperature.

6   On a large work surface, lay out two sheets of heavy-duty aluminum foil, each about 3 feet long, overlapping the sheets slightly along their longer sides. Place the roast in the center of the foil, fat side up. Fold up the edges to wrap the roast tightly to trap the steam. Return the roast to the smoker and cook over INDIRECT VERY LOW HEAT, with the lid closed, until the internal temperature reaches 190°F, at least 3 hours and as long as 5 hours. Remove from the smoker and let rest, still in the foil, for 1 hour.

7   In a medium, heavy-bottomed saucepan whisk the sauce ingredients including ¾ teaspoon salt. Bring to a simmer over medium heat and cook for about 5 minutes, stirring occasionally. Set aside.

8   Unwrap the roast and, when cool enough to handle, pull the meat apart to shred it. Discard any large pieces of fat and sinew. In a large saucepan over low heat, moisten the pork with as much sauce as you like and cook until warmed through, stirring occasionally. Pile the pulled pork on buns and top with coleslaw, such as Sweet and Tangy Vegetable Slaw (for the recipe, see page 180). Serve with any additional sauce.

SLOW-ROASTED HAM
WITH SWEET-AND-SOUR CIDER GLAZE

IDEAL
GRILL:

SMOKE INTENSITY: strong

PREP TIME: 15 minutes

COOKING TIME: 1¼ to 2 hours

SPECIAL EQUIPMENT: large disposable
foil pan, instant-read thermometer

SERVES: 10 to 12

1 whole, fully cooked, bone-in smoked
   ham, 8 to 10 pounds (not spiral cut)

4 large handfuls apple wood chips,
   soaked in water for at least 30 minutes

GLAZE
½ cup cider vinegar
½ cup ketchup
¼ cup fresh lime juice
3 tablespoons packed dark brown sugar
2 tablespoons soy sauce
1 tablespoon Dijon mustard
½ teaspoon ground black pepper

To prevent the ham from drying out, keep some water in the pan at all times. Whenever you add more briquettes to the fire, check to see if the pan needs another one-half cup or so.

1 Allow the ham to stand at room temperature for about 30 minutes before cooking.

2 Prepare a two-zone fire for low heat (250° to 350°F) (see pages 18–19).

3 Brush the cooking grate clean. Drain and add two handfuls of the wood chips to the charcoal and put the lid on the grill. Put the ham, flat side down, in a large disposable foil pan and add 1 cup of water. When the wood begins to smoke, place the pan on the cooking grate over INDIRECT LOW HEAT. Cook the ham, with the lid closed as much as possible, until an instant-read thermometer inserted into the thickest part of the ham (not touching the bone) reaches 135°F, 1¼ to 2 hours (about 10 minutes per pound). Replenish the charcoal as needed to maintain a steady temperature, adding three to five lit briquettes to each pile every 45 minutes, along with the remaining drained wood chips. Meanwhile, make the glaze.

4 In a small saucepan combine the glaze ingredients and simmer over medium heat until heated through, 3 to 4 minutes. Remove from the heat.

5 Glaze the ham during the last 30 minutes of cooking time. If the ham begins to look too dark, cover it with foil and stop glazing. Carefully transfer the ham from the foil pan to a cutting board. Tent with foil and let rest for 15 to 20 minutes. Cut the ham into slices and serve warm.

SAGE-SMOKED FRESH HAM
BASTED WITH MAPLE SYRUP

IDEAL
GRILL:

SMOKE INTENSITY: strong

PREP TIME: 30 minutes

COOKING TIME: about 5½ hours

SPECIAL EQUIPMENT:
large disposable foil pan, butcher's
twine, instant-read thermometer

SERVES: 14

RUB

1 ounce fresh sage sprigs
1 tablespoon kosher salt
1 teaspoon ground black pepper

½ fresh ham, preferably the shank
   end, about 9 pounds, rind removed
   (if attached), and fat trimmed to a
   thin layer
1 tablespoon vegetable oil

5 large handfuls apple wood chips
   (1 handful left dry; 4 handfuls soaked
   in water for at least 30 minutes)

½ cup maple syrup, preferably
   Grade B, divided

Maple syrup is sold in grades. Grade
A (or Grade 1) has several sub-gradations
and is suitable for pancakes or waffles.
Grade B (or Grade 2) is darker, stronger,
thicker, and better for cooking, smoking,
and grilling.

1 Remove and roughly chop enough sage leaves from the sprigs to measure 2 tablespoons. Add the salt and pepper and chop until the sage is minced. Scrape into a small bowl. Reserve the remaining sage sprigs.

2 Making cuts about 1 inch apart, lightly score the ham fat with a thin, sharp knife. Tie a few loops of butcher's twine around the circumference of the ham to help keep its shape during cooking. Brush the ham with the oil and season with the rub, pressing the spices into the meat. Allow the ham to stand at room temperature for 15 to 30 minutes before cooking.

3 Carefully place a large disposable foil pan underneath the cooking grates to catch the drippings. Prepare the grill for indirect cooking over low heat (250° to 350°F) (see pages 22–23). Place the dry wood chips in the smoker box of a gas grill, following manufacturer's instructions, and let them ignite and smolder.

4 Brush the cooking grates clean. Drain and add a handful of wood chips to the smoldering chips in the smoker box. Center the ham over the foil pan and cook over INDIRECT LOW HEAT, with the lid closed, for 4 hours. Keep the grill temperature as close to 325°F as possible. After every hour, add another handful of drained wood chips to the smoker box.

5 After 4 hours, place one-half of the sage sprigs and the final addition of drained wood chips into the smoker box. Baste the ham with ¼ cup of the syrup. Close the lid and continue cooking over INDIRECT LOW HEAT for 30 minutes.

6 Baste the ham with the remaining ¼ cup syrup and add the remaining sage sprigs to the smoker box. Continue cooking until an instant-read thermometer inserted into the center of the ham (not touching the bone) registers 160°F, about 1 hour more. During the last 15 minutes, increase the temperature of the grill to medium heat (350° to 450°F) to deepen the color of the glaze. Transfer the ham to a cutting board and let rest for about 15 minutes. Cut the ham into thin slices and serve warm.

APPLE-BRINED PORK RIB ROAST
WITH CRANBERRY SAUCE

IDEAL
GRILL:

SMOKE INTENSITY: strong

PREP TIME: 20 minutes

BRINING TIME: 4 to 5 hours

COOKING TIME: 3½ to 4 hours

SPECIAL EQUIPMENT:
instant-read thermometer

SERVES: 8

BRINE
- 2 lemons
- 2 quarts chilled unsweetened apple juice, divided
- ½ cup kosher salt
- ½ cup soy sauce
- 3 ounces fresh ginger, peeled and thinly sliced
- 1 tablespoon dried rosemary
- 1 teaspoon black peppercorns
- 2 bay leaves

- 1 bone-in pork rib roast, about 4½ pounds

- 6 fist-sized apple or hickory wood chunks

SAUCE
- 1 bag (12 ounces) fresh or frozen cranberries
- ⅔ cup honey
- ½ cup unsweetened apple juice *or* fresh orange juice *or* water
- 1 Granny Smith apple, peeled, cored, and cut into ½-inch dice
- 3 tablespoons calvados *or* applejack

Make sure the butcher removes the chine bone, the thick piece of the backbone attached to the ribs. This will allow you to cut the roast between the bones into individual chops.

1 Use a vegetable peeler to remove the zest in wide strips from the lemons. Put the zest in a medium saucepan with 1 quart of the apple juice, the salt, soy sauce, ginger, rosemary, peppercorns, and bay leaves. Bring to a simmer to release their flavors, stirring occasionally. Pour into a nonreactive, heatproof bowl set in a larger bowl of iced water. Let stand until chilled, about 30 minutes, stirring often. Stir the remaining chilled apple juice into the brine.

2 Put the roast in the brine, cover, and refrigerate for 4 to 5 hours. Remove the roast from the brine and rinse under cold water. Pat dry with paper towels. Allow the roast to stand at room temperature for about 30 minutes before cooking.

3 Prepare the smoker for indirect cooking with very low heat (200° to 250°F) (see pages 20–21). When the temperature reaches 225°F, add three wood chunks to the charcoal.

4 Brush the cooking grate clean. Smoke the roast over INDIRECT VERY LOW HEAT, with the lid closed as much as possible, until the internal temperature reaches 150°F, 3½ to 4 hours, adding the remaining three wood chunks after the first hour and additional lit briquettes as necessary to maintain the temperature inside the smoker. Remove the roast from the smoker and let rest for about 10 minutes (the internal temperature will rise 5 to 10 degrees during this time). While the pork rests, make the sauce.

5 In a medium saucepan over medium-high heat, combine the cranberries, honey, and apple juice and bring to a simmer. Reduce the heat to medium and cook until the juices are syrupy, about 7 minutes, stirring often. Stir in the apple and the calvados. Cook until the apple is crisp-tender, about 5 minutes, stirring often. The sauce can be served warm or at room temperature. (The sauce will thicken as it cools.)

6 Cut the roast between the bones into individual chops. Serve warm with the sauce.

SMOKED ROSEMARY PORK RIB ROAST
WITH CREAMY SAUERKRAUT

IDEAL GRILL:

SMOKE INTENSITY: moderate

PREP TIME: 20 minutes

MARINATING TIME: 30 minutes

COOKING TIME: 1¼ to 1½ hours

SPECIAL EQUIPMENT:
instant-read thermometer

SERVES: 4

MARINADE

- 3 tablespoons extra-virgin olive oil
- 2 tablespoons dry white wine
- 2 tablespoons finely chopped fresh rosemary leaves
- 1 tablespoon finely chopped fresh thyme leaves
- 1 teaspoon kosher salt
- ½ teaspoon ground black pepper

- 1 bone-in pork rib roast, about 3 pounds

- 4 large handfuls hickory or oak wood chips, soaked in water for at least 30 minutes

SAUERKRAUT

- 2 slices bacon, finely chopped
- 1 medium yellow onion, finely chopped
- 2 cups bottled or canned sauerkraut, rinsed
- 1 cup low-sodium chicken broth
- ½ cup dry white wine
- ⅓ cup heavy whipping cream
  Kosher salt
  Ground black pepper
  Freshly grated nutmeg

  Boiled new potatoes (optional)

When purchasing the pork loin, make sure to get a roast with at least four bones so that each person will have a nice thick pork chop with a rib bone attached. Ask the butcher to remove the chine bone (backbone) so that after the roast is cooked, you can cut between the rib bones easily.

1 In a medium bowl whisk the marinade ingredients. Spread about half of the marinade all over the roast. Reserve the remaining marinade for basting later. Allow the roast to marinate at room temperature for 30 minutes before cooking.

2 Prepare the grill for indirect cooking over medium heat (350° to 450°F).

3 Brush the cooking grates clean. Drain and add two handfuls of the wood chips to the smoker box of a gas grill, following manufacturer's instructions, and close the lid. When smoke begins to pour out of the grill, cook the roast, bone side down, over INDIRECT MEDIUM HEAT, with the lid closed, for 30 minutes. Keep the temperature of the grill as close to 350°F as possible.

4 After 30 minutes baste the roast with the reserved marinade and drain and add the remaining wood chips to the smoker box. Continue to cook, with the lid closed, until the internal temperature reaches 150°F, 45 minutes to 1 hour more. While the roast is cooking, prepare the sauerkraut.

5 In a medium saucepan over medium heat, brown the bacon for 4 to 6 minutes, stirring occasionally. Remove the bacon from the saucepan. Add the onion to the saucepan and cook until tender, 4 to 6 minutes, stirring occasionally. Add the sauerkraut, broth, wine, and cream and season with salt, pepper, and nutmeg. Simmer until most of the liquid has evaporated and the sauerkraut reaches your desired consistency, 15 to 20 minutes. Remove the saucepan from the heat. Stir in the bacon.

6 When the roast is done, transfer it to a cutting board and let rest for 10 to 15 minutes (the internal temperature will rise 5 to 10 degrees during this time). Warm the sauerkraut over medium heat. Cut the roast between the bones. Serve the pork chops warm with sauerkraut and boiled new potatoes, if desired.

5

Poultry

SMOKED DUCK AND CHERRY SAUSAGES

IDEAL GRILL:

SMOKE INTENSITY: mild

PREP TIME: 1½ hours

FREEZING TIME: 3 hours

REFRIGERATION TIME: 24 hours

COOKING TIME: about 25 minutes

SPECIAL EQUIPMENT: meat grinder, sausage stuffing equipment, instant-read thermometer

SERVES: 6 to 8 (makes 12 sausages, each about 5 inches long)

2 pounds boneless, skinless duck meat, cut into 1-inch chunks (from 2 whole 5-pound ducks or 8 duck breasts or 4 pounds duck leg quarters)
12 ounces pork belly, rind removed, cut into 1-inch chunks

½ cup roughly chopped dried tart cherries
¼ cup tawny port, chilled
¼ cup ice-cold water
2½ teaspoons kosher salt
2½ teaspoons ground black pepper
1 teaspoon paprika
1 garlic clove, minced
½ teaspoon dried thyme
½ teaspoon dried sage
½ teaspoon pink curing salt
¼ teaspoon ground allspice

4 feet prepared hog casing, soaked in cold water for 30 minutes
Vegetable oil
1 large handful hickory wood chips, soaked in water for at least 30 minutes

Cold temperature is the key to making sausage. If the meat gets warm at any point in the procedure, the fat softens and makes the sausage greasy. For this reason, the meat is frozen before grinding, the port and water are ice cold, and the sausage mixture sits in a bowl of ice while awaiting stuffing.

1 Spread the chunks of duck and pork belly on a large sheet pan. Freeze until frosty but not hard, about 2 hours. Remove from the freezer and grind the meat through the coarse blade of a meat grinder, or through the grinding attachment of a stand mixer, into a large, nonreactive bowl. Freeze for 1 hour.

2 Add the dried cherries, port, water, kosher salt, pepper, paprika, garlic, thyme, sage, pink curing salt, and allspice to the chilled ground meat. Mix well with a large spoon. Place the bowl in a larger bowl of ice water to keep it cold throughout the stuffing process.

3 Rinse the casings several times by running cold water inside the entire length of the casing. Attach the sausage stuffing equipment to a stand mixer according to manufacturer's instructions. Lubricate the tip of the stuffer tube with oil and slide the casing onto the stuffer tube. Tie the end of the casing. Push the meat mixture through the stuffer tube, forcing it into the casing. After you have a five-inch sausage, twist the casing a couple times and then create another sausage. Keep going until all the meat is used. You will be able to make about 12 sausages. Knot the open end of the casing. Roll the sausage rope into a spiral and place it on a sheet pan. Cover with plastic wrap and refrigerate for 24 hours to blend the flavors.

4 Prepare a two-zone fire for medium heat (350° to 450°F) (see pages 18–19).

5 Pierce each sausage link a few times with the tip of a skewer or once with a dinner fork. Brush the cooking grate clean. Drain and add the wood chips to the charcoal and put the lid on the grill. When smoke appears, cook the sausage rope over INDIRECT MEDIUM HEAT, with the lid closed, until an instant-read thermometer inserted into the center of one sausage reaches 165°F, about 25 minutes. Remove from the grill and cut into individual links. Serve right away.

If you want to skip the stuffing altogether, shape the sausage mixture into eight patties, each about 5 inches in diameter. Lightly brush the patties with oil. Cook over INDIRECT MEDIUM HEAT, with the lid closed, until firm, about 20 minutes (do not turn). Then move over DIRECT MEDIUM HEAT and cook until lightly browned on both sides, about 3 minutes, turning once. The patties are great on their own, but they also make excellent burgers.

TEA-SMOKED DUCK BREASTS
WITH SWEET SOY DIPPING SAUCE

IDEAL
GRILL:

SMOKE INTENSITY: moderate

PREP TIME: 15 minutes

COOKING TIME: 10 to 11 minutes

SPECIAL EQUIPMENT: large disposable
foil pan, 12-inch cast-iron skillet

SERVES: 4

*Like wood chips, dried tea and brown
sugar release aromatic smoke, but by
themselves they tend to burn out quickly.
Adding rice to the mixture extends
the length of time for the tea and sugar
to smolder.*

RUB
1½ teaspoons Chinese five spice
1½ teaspoons garlic powder
½ teaspoon kosher salt

4 duck breast halves, each 4 to 6 ounces

¼ cup loose-leaf black tea
3 tablespoons packed light brown sugar
¼ cup white rice (short, medium, or
long grain)

SAUCE
⅓ cup fresh lemon juice
¼ cup soy sauce
2 tablespoons honey

1 Prepare a two-zone fire for medium heat (350° to 450°F) (see pages 18–19). Place a large disposable foil pan beside the bed of charcoal and fill three-quarters of the way full with water.

2 In a small bowl mix the rub ingredients. Using a sharp knife, score the skin of each duck breast on the diagonal in a crisscross pattern (do not cut through the breast meat). Season the duck evenly on both sides with the rub. In a small bowl combine the tea, brown sugar, and rice. Pour this mixture down the center of a 12-by-20-inch sheet of heavy-duty aluminum foil. Fold the long sides over the mixture, and then loosely fold in the shorter ends to create a packet.

3 In a small, nonreactive bowl combine the sauce ingredients. Set aside.

4 Brush the cooking grate clean. Preheat a 12-inch cast-iron skillet over DIRECT MEDIUM HEAT for 5 minutes. Lay the duck in the skillet, skin side down, and sear until the skin is crisp and golden, 2 to 3 minutes. Remove the duck from the skillet and set aside. Wearing insulated barbecue mitts, carefully remove the skillet from the grill.

5 Place the tea packet, with the seam side up, directly on the charcoal. When the packet begins to smoke, place the duck breasts, skin side up, over INDIRECT MEDIUM HEAT above the pan of water. Close the lid and smoke the duck breasts until cooked to your desired doneness, about 8 minutes for medium. Remove from the grill and let rest for 3 to 5 minutes. Serve the duck warm with the sauce.

CHICKEN SOUVLAKI SANDWICHES
WITH TZATZIKI SAUCE

IDEAL GRILL:

SMOKE INTENSITY: moderate

PREP TIME: 25 minutes

CHILLING TIME: at least 1 hour

COOKING TIME: 9 to 13 minutes

SERVES: 6

TZATZIKI

- 1 cup plain Greek yogurt
- ½ large English cucumber, minced (about ⅔ cup)
- 2 tablespoons tahini
- 2 tablespoons fresh lemon juice
- 1 tablespoon finely chopped fresh dill
- 1 garlic clove, minced

    Kosher salt
    Ground black pepper

RUB

- 2 teaspoons ground cumin
- 2 teaspoons ground coriander

- 4 boneless, skinless chicken breast halves, each about 6 ounces
- 2 tablespoons extra-virgin olive oil

- 1 large handful oak wood chips, soaked in water for at least 30 minutes
- 6 whole-wheat pita pockets, tops cut off
- 2 cups shredded iceberg lettuce
- 3 ripe plum tomatoes, each cut into ¼-inch slices
- ½ red onion, thinly sliced

1 In a medium, nonreactive bowl combine the *tzatziki* ingredients. Season with salt and pepper. Cover and refrigerate for at least 1 hour or up to 1 day.

2 In a small bowl mix the rub ingredients, including ¾ teaspoon salt, and ½ teaspoon pepper. Brush the chicken breasts on both sides with the oil and season evenly with the rub.

3 Prepare a two-zone fire for medium heat (350° to 450°F) (see pages 18–19).

4 Brush the cooking grate clean. Drain and add the wood chips to the charcoal and put the lid on the grill. When the wood begins to smoke, cook the chicken, smooth (skin) side down first, over DIRECT MEDIUM HEAT, with the lid closed as much as possible, until the meat is firm to the touch and opaque all the way to the center, 8 to 12 minutes, turning once or twice. Remove from the grill and let rest for 3 to 5 minutes. Cut the chicken crosswise into ½-inch slices.

5 Grill the pita pockets over DIRECT MEDIUM HEAT, with the lid closed, until warmed, about 1 minute, turning once. Remove from the grill and fill with chicken, *tzatziki*, lettuce, tomatoes, and onion. Serve warm.

Leftover tzatziki *sauce makes an excellent dip for pita chips or raw vegetables. The sauce can be refrigerated for up to three days.*

HICKORY-BARBECUED CHICKEN

IDEAL
GRILL:

SMOKE INTENSITY: moderate

PREP TIME: 20 minutes

COOKING TIME: 41 to 45 minutes

SERVES: 4

RUB

2 teaspoons paprika
2 teaspoons kosher salt
½ teaspoon granulated garlic
½ teaspoon ground black pepper

4 whole chicken legs, each 10 to 12 ounces, cut into thighs and drumsticks

SAUCE

1 cup ketchup
¼ cup cider vinegar
1 tablespoon packed light brown sugar
1 tablespoon Dijon mustard
2 teaspoons hot pepper sauce

2 large handfuls hickory wood chips, soaked in water for at least 30 minutes

Grill the chicken with the skin side down first to melt the fat under the skin. This will help the skin develop a somewhat crispy texture, even when you brush the sauce all over it.

1 In a small bowl mix the rub ingredients. Season the chicken thighs and drumsticks all over with the rub.

2 Prepare the grill for direct and indirect cooking over medium heat (350° to 450°F) (see pages 22–23).

3 In a medium saucepan combine the sauce ingredients. Bring to a simmer over medium heat and cook until slightly thickened, 6 to 8 minutes, stirring occasionally.

4 Brush the cooking grates clean. Cook the chicken, skin side down first, over DIRECT MEDIUM HEAT, with the lid closed as much as possible, until golden brown, 6 to 10 minutes, turning occasionally. Move the chicken over INDIRECT MEDIUM HEAT. Drain and add the wood chips to the smoker box of a gas grill, following manufacturer's instructions. Close the lid and continue cooking until the juices run clear and the meat is opaque all the way to the bone, about 35 minutes, basting with the sauce and turning several times during the last 20 minutes of cooking time. Remove from the grill and let rest for 3 to 5 minutes. Serve warm or at room temperature with any remaining sauce on the side.

TANDOORI-MARINATED CHICKEN
WITH INDIAN CORN RELISH

IDEAL
GRILL:

SMOKE INTENSITY: strong

PREP TIME: 30 minutes

MARINATING TIME: 6 to 8 hours

COOKING TIME: about 1¼ hours

SPECIAL EQUIPMENT:
large disposable foil pan

SERVES: 6

MARINADE

1½ cups plain Greek yogurt
1 small yellow onion, chopped
2 tablespoons chopped fresh ginger
2 tablespoons fresh lemon juice
2 tablespoons curry powder
2 tablespoons paprika
4 garlic cloves, roughly chopped
¼ teaspoon ground cayenne pepper
   Kosher salt

6 whole chicken legs, each 10 to
   12 ounces, skin removed

RELISH

2 ears fresh corn, husked
3 plum tomatoes, seeded, cut into
   ½-inch dice
⅓ cup minced red onion
2 tablespoons minced fresh
   cilantro leaves
2 teaspoons peeled, minced fresh ginger
3 tablespoons cider vinegar
2 teaspoons granulated sugar
½ teaspoon ground cumin
½ teaspoon ground coriander
¼ teaspoon ground cinnamon
¼ teaspoon crushed red pepper flakes

2 large handfuls apple wood chips,
   soaked in water for at least 30 minutes

1 In a food processor combine the marinade ingredients, including 2 teaspoons salt, and process until smooth.

2 Put the chicken in a large glass baking dish. Pour the marinade over the chicken and turn to coat. Cover and refrigerate for 6 to 8 hours, turning once.

3 Prepare a two-zone fire for medium heat (350° to 450°F) (see pages 18–19).

4 Brush the cooking grate clean. Cook the corn over DIRECT MEDIUM HEAT, with the lid closed as much as possible, until browned in spots and tender, 10 to 12 minutes, turning occasionally. Remove from the grill and, when cool enough to handle, cut the kernels off the cobs. In a large, nonreactive bowl mix all of the relish ingredients. Season with ¼ teaspoon salt. Cover and refrigerate for at least 2 hours to blend the flavors.

5 Prepare a two-zone fire for high heat (450° to 550°F). Place a large disposable foil pan beside the bed of charcoal and fill three-quarters of the way full with water.

6 Remove the chicken from the dish (do not remove the marinade that clings to the chicken). Brush the cooking grate clean. Drain and add one handful of the wood chips to the charcoal and put the lid on the grill. When the wood begins to smoke, cook the chicken, bone side down, over INDIRECT HIGH HEAT, with the lid closed, until the juices run clear and the meat is no longer pink at the bone, about 1 hour. After 30 minutes of cooking time, drain and add the remaining wood chips to the charcoal. Remove the chicken from the grill and let rest for 3 to 5 minutes. Serve warm with the relish.

The chicken legs that you set closest to the charcoal are bound to cook faster than the others, so swap their positions once or twice for even cooking.

POMEGRANATE-GLAZED QUAIL
WITH DRIED CHERRIES AND WALNUTS

IDEAL GRILL:

SMOKE INTENSITY: moderate

PREP TIME: 20 minutes

MARINATING TIME: 8 to 24 hours

COOKING TIME: about 16 minutes

SERVES: 4

Many marinades (like this one) can double as salad dressings. However, note that some of the marinade is set aside for this purpose. Never use marinade that has come into contact with raw meat for a salad dressing.

MARINADE

- 3 tablespoons pomegranate molasses
- 3 tablespoons balsamic vinegar
- 2 teaspoons finely chopped fresh thyme leaves
- ¾ teaspoon kosher salt
- ½ teaspoon crushed red pepper flakes
- 1 cup extra-virgin olive oil

- 8 whole quail, backbones and wing tips removed, butterflied
  Kosher salt
  Ground black pepper
- 1 large handful oak wood chips, soaked in water for at least 30 minutes

SALAD

- 1 heart of romaine, cut crosswise into thin strips
- ½ cup roughly chopped dried tart cherries
- ½ cup coarsely chopped walnuts

1 In a small bowl whisk the molasses, vinegar, thyme, salt, and red pepper flakes. Gradually whisk in the oil. Pour ½ cup of the marinade into a small, nonreactive bowl to use for the salad. Cover and refrigerate until ready to use. Place the quail in a large resealable plastic bag and pour in the remaining marinade. Press the air out of the bag and seal tightly. Turn the bag to distribute the marinade, place in a bowl, and refrigerate for at least 8 hours or up to 24 hours, turning occasionally.

2 Prepare a two-zone fire for high heat (450° to 550°F) (see pages 18–19).

3 Remove the quail from the bag, letting the excess marinade drip back into the bag. Discard the marinade. Season the quail with 1 teaspoon salt and ½ teaspoon pepper. Brush the cooking grate clean. Drain and add the wood chips to the charcoal and put the lid on the grill. When smoke appears, cook the quail, breast side up, over **INDIRECT HIGH HEAT**, with the lid closed, until the meat shows no sign of pink when pierced with the tip of a knife at the thigh bone, about 15 minutes. To crisp the skin, move the quail over **DIRECT HIGH HEAT**, skin side down, and cook for about 1 minute, turning once. Remove from the grill.

4 In a large bowl toss the salad ingredients with the reserved, refrigerated marinade. Season with salt and pepper. Serve the quail warm with the salad.

BUTTERFLIED CURRY CHICKEN

IDEAL GRILL:

SMOKE INTENSITY: moderate

PREP TIME: 15 minutes

COOKING TIME: 1¾ to 2¼ hours

SPECIAL EQUIPMENT: poultry shears, instant-read thermometer

SERVES: 4

Whole chicken has such an uneven shape that it is challenging to cook it evenly. Butterflying the chicken helps a lot, as it creates a relatively even shape. Cooking the chicken slowly also helps.

RUB

- 1 tablespoon granulated sugar
- 1 tablespoon kosher salt
- 1 tablespoon curry powder
- ½ teaspoon granulated garlic
- ¼ teaspoon ground cayenne pepper

- 1 whole chicken, about 5 pounds, giblets and any excess fat removed

- 4 large handfuls apple wood chips, soaked in water for at least 30 minutes

- ¼ cup (½ stick) unsalted butter, melted

1 In a small bowl combine the rub ingredients. Place the chicken, breast side down, on a cutting board. Using poultry shears, cut from the neck to the tail end, along either side of the backbone. Remove the backbone. Once the backbone is out, you'll be able to see the interior of the chicken. Make a small slit in the cartilage at the bottom end of the breastbone. Then, placing both hands on the rib cage, crack the chicken open like a book. Run your fingers along either side of the cartilage in between the breast to loosen it from the flesh. Grab the bone and pull up on it to remove it along with the attached cartilage. The chicken should now lie flat. Season the chicken evenly on all sides with the rub.

2 Prepare the grill for indirect cooking over low heat (250° to 350°F) (see pages 22–23).

3 Brush the cooking grates clean. When the temperature of the grill reaches 325°F, drain and add two handfuls of the wood chips to the smoker box of a gas grill, following manufacturer's instructions, and close the lid. When the wood begins to smoke, cook the chicken, bone side down, over **INDIRECT LOW HEAT**, with the lid closed, until the juices run clear and an instant-read thermometer inserted into the thickest part of the thigh (not touching the bone) reaches 160° to 165°F, 1¾ to 2¼ hours. Lightly brush the chicken with melted butter every 30 minutes, and drain and add the remaining wood chips to the smoker box after the first 30 minutes. When the chicken is done, remove it from the grill and let rest for 5 to 10 minutes (the internal temperature will rise 5 to 10 degrees during this time).

4 Cut the chicken into serving pieces. Serve warm.

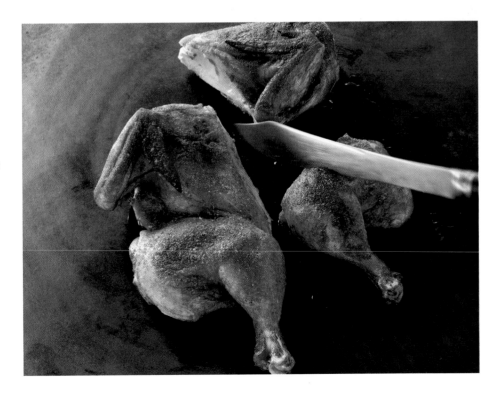

MESQUITE BEER CAN CHICKEN

IDEAL GRILL:

SMOKE INTENSITY: moderate

PREP TIME: 15 minutes

COOKING TIME: 1¼ to 1½ hours

SPECIAL EQUIPMENT: large disposable foil pan, instant-read thermometer

SERVES: 4

RUB

- 1 teaspoon granulated garlic
- 1 teaspoon prepared chili powder
- 1 teaspoon kosher salt
- ½ teaspoon ground black pepper

- 1 whole chicken, 4 to 5 pounds, giblets and any excess fat removed
  Extra-virgin olive oil

- 1 can (12 fluid ounces) beer, at room temperature
- 4 large handfuls mesquite wood chips, soaked in water for at least 30 minutes

If standing a whole chicken on a beer can sounds wacky to you, put aside your skepticism for a moment and think about how tender and juicy the chicken will be when it is cooked from the inside with steaming beer. Then imagine what the aromatic wood smoke will do to flavor the spice-rubbed skin. Now you have some idea of why this technique has achieved legendary status in the world of American barbecue. The trickiest part of the process may be getting the hot can out of the chicken. To do so, get a good grip on the neck and back of the chicken with tongs, lift the chicken up, and then, using another pair of tongs, pull out the can.

1 Prepare a two-zone fire for medium heat (350° to 450°F) (see pages 18–19). Place a large disposable foil pan beside the bed of charcoal and fill three-quarters of the way full with water.

2 In a small bowl mix the rub ingredients. Lightly coat the chicken all over with oil and season evenly with the rub. Fold the wing tips behind the chicken's back.

3 Open the can of beer and pour out about half. Using a can opener, make two more holes in the top of the can. Place the can on a solid surface, and then lower the chicken cavity over the can.

4 Brush the cooking grate clean. Drain and add the wood chips to the charcoal and put the lid on the grill. When the wood begins to smoke, transfer the chicken-on-a-can to the grill, balancing it on its two legs and the can, like a tripod. Cook the chicken over INDIRECT MEDIUM HEAT, with the lid closed, until the juices run clear and the internal temperature registers 160° to 165°F in the thickest part of the thigh (not touching the bone), 1¼ to 1½ hours. Replenish the charcoal as needed to maintain a steady temperature, adding 6 to 10 lit briquettes after 45 minutes.

5 Carefully remove the chicken-on-a-can from the grill (do not spill the contents of the beer can, as it will be very hot). Let rest for 5 to 10 minutes (the internal temperature will rise 5 to 10 degrees during this time) before lifting it from the can and cutting it into serving pieces. Serve warm.

WHOLE ROASTED DUCK
WITH PINEAPPLE CHUTNEY

IDEAL
GRILL:

SMOKE INTENSITY: moderate

PREP TIME: 30 minutes

STEAMING TIME: about 1½ hours

COOLING TIME: 1 hour

REFRIGERATION TIME: 12 to 24 hours

COOKING TIME: about 1 hour

SPECIAL EQUIPMENT:
roasting rack, 3 large disposable foil
pans, instant-read thermometer

SERVES: 4

1 whole duck, about 6 pounds, giblets,
   neck, and wing tips removed
2 teaspoons kosher salt
½ teaspoon ground black pepper
2 whole star anise
1 cinnamon stick, about 3 inches long

CHUTNEY
1 pound peeled, cored fresh pineapple,
   cut into ¼-inch dice
¼ cup packed light brown sugar
¼ cup finely chopped red onion
3 tablespoons unseasoned rice vinegar
1½ tablespoons peeled, minced
   fresh ginger
1 whole star anise
1 cinnamon stick, about 3 inches long
¼ teaspoon seeded, minced Thai *or*
   serrano chile pepper

4 large handfuls cherry wood chips,
   soaked in water for at least 30 minutes

Steaming the duck helps melt some of the excess fat from its skin. Refrigerating the duck overnight dries and tightens the skin to help it release even more fat during cooking.

1 Using a meat fork, pierce the duck skin all over, especially the breast and thigh areas, taking care not to pierce the flesh. Season the duck inside and outside with the salt and pepper. Put the star anise and the cinnamon stick inside the body cavity.

2 Preheat the oven to 350°F. Place the duck on a roasting rack and set it inside a large disposable foil pan. Add 1 quart of warm water to the pan. Invert another foil pan and use it to cover the duck. Steam the duck, covered, in the oven, until the skin shrinks around the legs and thighs and most of the fat has rendered out, about 1½ hours. Remove from the oven and let cool at room temperature for 1 hour. Refrigerate the cooled duck, uncovered, for 12 to 24 hours.

3 In a medium saucepan over medium heat, bring the chutney ingredients to a simmer. Cook until the pineapple is translucent and the chutney has reduced to about 1 cup, about 20 minutes, stirring often. Transfer to a nonreactive bowl and remove the star anise and the cinnamon stick. Let cool.

4 Prepare a two-zone fire for medium heat (350° to 450°F) (see pages 18–19). Place a large disposable foil pan beside the bed of charcoal and fill three-quarters of the way full with water.

5 Brush the cooking grate clean. Drain and add two handfuls of the wood chips to the charcoal and put the lid on the grill. When the wood begins to smoke, cook the duck over INDIRECT MEDIUM HEAT, with the lid closed, for 30 minutes. Drain and add the remaining wood chips to the charcoal. Continue cooking, with the lid closed, until an instant-read thermometer inserted into the thickest part of the thigh (not touching the bone) registers 170°F, about 30 minutes more. If desired, move the duck over DIRECT MEDIUM HEAT to crisp the skin for a few minutes, turning occasionally, but be careful that the skin does not burn. Remove from the grill and let rest for about 15 minutes (the internal temperature will rise 5 to 10 degrees during this time).

6 Cut the duck into serving pieces and serve hot with the chutney.

BARBECUED TURKEY DRUMSTICKS

WITH CHILE DRY RUB

IDEAL GRILL:

SMOKE INTENSITY: **strong**

PREP TIME: **15 minutes**

BRINING TIME: **2 hours**

COOKING TIME: **about 3 hours**

SPECIAL EQUIPMENT:
instant-read thermometer

SERVES: **8**

BRINE

- 3 bottles (each 12 fluid ounces) lager
- 3½ cups water
- ½ cup kosher salt
- ½ cup packed light brown sugar

- 8 turkey drumsticks or thighs, each about 12 ounces

RUB

- ¼ cup pure chile powder
- 2 teaspoons dried oregano
- 1 teaspoon granulated garlic
- 1 teaspoon ground cumin

- 6 small mesquite wood chunks

Turkey drumsticks and thighs, both dark meat cuts, work equally well with this recipe. Turkey thighs are often more difficult to find at the market, but the meat is easy to cut off the bone in large chunks.

1 In a wide, nonreactive pot stir the brine ingredients until the salt and sugar are dissolved. Put the turkey drumsticks in the brine and then place a plate on top to keep them submerged. Cover and refrigerate for 2 hours.

2 In a small bowl mix the rub ingredients.

3 Prepare the smoker for indirect cooking with very low heat (200° to 250°F) (see pages 20–21). When the temperature reaches 225°F, add two of the wood chunks to the charcoal.

4 Remove the drumsticks from the pot and discard the brine. Rinse them under cold running water and pat dry with paper towels. Coat the drumsticks with the rub.

5 Brush the cooking grate clean. Smoke the drumsticks over **INDIRECT VERY LOW HEAT**, with the lid closed, until the skin is dark brown, the meat is tender at the bone, and an instant-read thermometer inserted into the thickest part of the drumstick (not touching the bone) registers 180°F, about 3 hours. After the first and second hours, add two more wood chunks and more lit briquettes as necessary to maintain the heat.

6 Remove the drumsticks from the smoker and let rest for 5 to 10 minutes. Serve warm.

SMOKED TURKEY BREAST
WITH HONEY MUSTARD

IDEAL
GRILL:

SMOKE INTENSITY: strong

PREP TIME: 15 minutes

BRINING TIME: 5 hours

REFRIGERATION TIME: 12 to 16 hours

COOKING TIME: about 4 hours

SPECIAL EQUIPMENT:
instant-read thermometer

SERVES: 8

BRINE
2 quarts water
½ cup kosher salt
½ cup honey
2 teaspoons dried rosemary
2 teaspoons dried sage
1½ teaspoons dried marjoram
1 teaspoon black peppercorns
2 bay leaves

1 whole turkey breast (with bone and skin), about 5½ pounds

MUSTARD
½ cup Dijon mustard
3 tablespoons honey
2 tablespoons packed light brown sugar

8 small apple wood chunks

Be sure to use a fresh turkey breast for brining. Most frozen turkey breasts are injected with a sodium solution to replace the juices lost during the freezing process. If you brine a turkey breast that has already been treated with salt, you are essentially brining a product that has already been salted. The result could be way too salty.

1 In a large, nonreactive pot whisk the brine ingredients until the salt is dissolved. Put the turkey breast in the brine. Put a plate on top of the turkey breast to keep it submerged, cover, and refrigerate for 5 hours.

2 Remove the turkey breast from the pot and discard the brine. Rinse under cold running water and pat dry with paper towels. Place on a wire rack set over a rimmed sheet pan. Refrigerate, uncovered, for 12 to 16 hours to dry the skin.

3 Prepare the smoker for indirect cooking with very low heat (200° to 250°F) (see pages 20–21). When the temperature reaches 225°F, add two wood chunks to the charcoal.

4 In a small bowl mix the mustard ingredients until the brown sugar is dissolved. Cover and set aside at room temperature until ready to serve.

5 Brush the cooking grate clean. Smoke the turkey over INDIRECT VERY LOW HEAT, with the lid closed, until the skin is dark brown, the meat is tender at the bone, and an instant-read meat thermometer inserted into the thickest part of the breast (not touching the bone) reaches 160° to 165°F, about 4 hours. After the first, second, and third hours, add two more wood chunks and more lit briquettes as necessary to maintain the heat. Remove from the smoker and let rest for 5 to 10 minutes (the internal temperature will rise 5 to 10 degrees during this time).

6 Carve the turkey breast into thin slices. Serve warm with the honey mustard on the side.

APPLE-SMOKED TURKEY
WITH APPLEJACK GRAVY

IDEAL GRILL:

SMOKE INTENSITY: moderate

PREP TIME: 45 minutes

COOKING TIME: 3 to 3½ hours

SPECIAL EQUIPMENT:
2 large disposable foil pans, roasting rack, instant-read thermometer, gravy separator

SERVES: 8 to 12

BUTTER

- 6 tablespoons (¾ stick) unsalted butter, softened
- 2 teaspoons dried rosemary
- 2 teaspoons dried sage
- 2 teaspoons dried thyme
- ½ teaspoon granulated garlic
- ½ teaspoon granulated onion

- 1 whole turkey, about 13 pounds, thawed if necessary
  Kosher salt
  Ground black pepper
- 1 small onion, about 6 ounces, peeled and quartered
- 1 tart apple, such as Granny Smith, about 6 ounces, cored and quartered
- 3 cups low-sodium chicken broth *or* turkey broth

- 6 large handfuls apple wood chips, soaked in water for at least 30 minutes

GRAVY

- 1–2 cups low-sodium chicken broth *or* turkey broth, if needed
- 3 tablespoons unsalted butter, melted, if needed
- ½ cup all-purpose flour
- ¼ cup applejack

Do not use a high-quality metal roasting pan, as the smoke may discolor it.

1 In a small bowl mix the butter ingredients.

2 Remove the giblets and neck from the turkey and reserve for another use. Remove and discard the pop-up timer if there is one. Rinse the turkey, inside and outside, under cold water and pat dry with paper towels. Tuck the wing tips behind the turkey's back. Generously rub the turkey with the herb butter and then season evenly, inside and outside, with 1 tablespoon salt and 1 teaspoon pepper. Stuff the turkey with the onion and apple. Cover the entire turkey breast with aluminum foil, but don't cover the wings or thighs.

3 Place one large disposable foil pan inside the other. Pour 3 cups of broth into the top pan. Place the turkey on a roasting rack, breast side down, and set it inside the pans. Let the turkey stand at room temperature for 1 hour before cooking.

4 Prepare the grill for indirect cooking over low heat (250° to 350°F).

5 Brush the cooking grates clean. Drain and add two handfuls of wood chips to the smoker box of a gas grill, following manufacturer's instructions, and close the lid. When the wood begins to smoke, cook the turkey in the pans over INDIRECT LOW HEAT, with the lid closed, for 45 minutes. Drain and add another two handfuls of wood chips to the smoker box, and continue cooking the turkey for 45 minutes more.

6 After 1½ hours, wearing insulated barbecue mitts and using a pair of tongs, turn the turkey over so that the breast side is facing up. Remove and discard the foil. Drain and add the remaining two handfuls of wood chips to the smoker box. Continue cooking the turkey until it is golden brown and an instant-read thermometer inserted in the thickest part of the thigh (not touching the bone) reaches 170° to 175°F, 1½ to 2 hours more.

7 Carefully remove the turkey and the pans from the grill. Tilt the turkey so the juices run out of the body cavity and into the pans. Transfer the turkey to a cutting board and let rest for 20 to 30 minutes (the internal temperature will rise 5 to 10 degrees during this time). Save the pan juices to make the gravy.

8 Strain the pan juices into a gravy separator. Let stand until the fat rises to the surface, about 3 minutes. Pour the juices into a 1-quart measuring cup, reserving the fat. Add more broth as needed to make 1 quart.

9 Measure the fat. You should have ½ cup. Add melted butter if needed. In a medium saucepan over medium heat, heat the fat (and butter). Whisk in the flour and let bubble for 1 minute, stirring constantly. Whisk in the pan juices and the applejack. Bring to a simmer, whisking often. Reduce the heat to medium-low and simmer until lightly thickened, 5 to 10 minutes. Remove from the heat and season with salt and pepper.

10 Carve the turkey and serve warm with the gravy.

6

Seafood

NEW ENGLAND CLAMBAKE

IDEAL GRILL:

SMOKE INTENSITY: moderate

PREP TIME: 30 minutes

COOKING TIME: about 45 minutes

SPECIAL EQUIPMENT:
large disposable foil pan

SERVES: 4

1½ pounds baby new potatoes
   (about 2 dozen)
1 tablespoon plus 2 teaspoons
   extra-virgin olive oil, divided
4 ears fresh corn, husked
1 cup (2 sticks) unsalted butter,
   cut into pieces
4 dozen littleneck clams, rinsed
   and scrubbed
¾ cup lager
4 lobster tails, each about 4 ounces,
   cut in half lengthwise
1 pound extra-large shrimp (16/20
   count), deveined, shells and tails
   left on
1 large handful alder or maple wood
   chips, soaked in water for at least
   30 minutes
   Kosher salt
   Ground black pepper
2 lemons, each cut into quarters

🔥 *To prepare the lobster tails, use kitchen scissors to cut through the center of the shell on the underside of each tail. Turn each tail over and cut through the harder back shell all the way to the fins. Cut each tail in half lengthwise, passing through the openings you have already made.*

1 Prepare a two-zone fire for high heat (450° to 550°F) (see pages 18–19). Preheat the oven to 200°F.

2 In a large bowl toss the potatoes with 1 tablespoon of the oil. Wrap the potatoes in heavy-duty aluminum foil and create a packet, crimping the edges tightly. Wrap each ear of corn in foil.

3 Cook the packet of potatoes over DIRECT HIGH HEAT, with the lid closed as much as possible, for 20 minutes. Carefully turn the packet over, being careful not to puncture the foil, and then place the corn on the cooking grate. Continue to cook over DIRECT HIGH HEAT, with the lid closed as much as possible, until the potatoes and corn are tender, about 15 minutes, turning the corn three or four times. Transfer the potato packet and corn to a large sheet pan and place in the oven to keep warm.

4 Arrange the coals in a bull's-eye configuration (see photo at bottom left), adding enough charcoal briquettes to raise the temperature of the grill back up to high heat. Let the charcoal burn until covered with white ash, about 15 minutes.

5 Meanwhile, in a small, heavy saucepan over medium heat, cook the butter until melted and boiling. Pour the melted butter into a glass measuring cup and let stand for 5 minutes. Skim the foam from the surface. Pour the butter into four individual ramekins, leaving the milky residue at the bottom of the measuring cup. Transfer the ramekins to the sheet pan in the oven to keep warm.

6 Put the clams in a large disposable foil pan and pour in the lager. Cover tightly with aluminum foil. Brush the lobster flesh and the shrimp with the remaining 2 teaspoons oil.

7 Brush the cooking grates clean. Drain and add the wood chips to the charcoal and put the lid on the grill. When the wood begins to smoke, place the foil pan with the clams over DIRECT HIGH HEAT. Place the lobster, meat side down, and the shrimp over INDIRECT HIGH HEAT. Close the lid and cook until the clams have opened, the lobster meat is white and firm but not dry, and the shrimp are firm to the touch and just turning opaque in the center, shaking the foil pan after 5 minutes to redistribute the clams and turning the lobster and the shrimp once or twice. The clams and lobster will take about 10 minutes and the shrimp will take 3 to 5 minutes. Remove from the grill as they are done.

8 Place the potatoes, corn, and clams in separate serving bowls and the lobster and shrimp on a platter. Season the potatoes and corn with salt and pepper as desired. Serve at once with the melted butter and lemon quarters.

SMOKY SHRIMP TACOS
WITH CHIPOTLE CREMA

IDEAL GRILL:

SMOKE INTENSITY: moderate

PREP TIME: 20 minutes

COOKING TIME: 5 to 7 minutes

SPECIAL EQUIPMENT:
perforated grill pan

SERVES: 4

CREMA
1   canned chipotle chile pepper in adobo sauce, stemmed, seeded, and chopped
1½   teaspoons adobo sauce from the canned chipotles
½   teaspoon minced garlic
½   cup sour cream

1   small head romaine lettuce, about 7 ounces, cored and shredded
2   ripe medium tomatoes, seeded and diced
⅓   English cucumber, diced
½   cup tightly packed fresh cilantro leaves

1   tablespoon extra-virgin olive oil
½   teaspoon kosher salt
¼   teaspoon ground black pepper
1   pound medium shrimp (31/35 count), peeled and deveined, tails removed

1   large handful mesquite wood chips, soaked in water for at least 30 minutes

12   corn or flour tortillas (6 inches)
2   limes, cut into wedges
    Pickled jalapeño rings (optional)

1   Prepare a two-zone fire for medium heat (350° to 450°F) (see pages 18–19) and preheat the grill pan on the cooking grate.

2   In a small bowl using the back of a spoon, mash the chile, adobo sauce, and garlic into a paste. Stir in the sour cream.

3   In a large bowl combine the lettuce, tomatoes, cucumber, and cilantro. Cover and refrigerate until ready to use.

4   In a medium bowl whisk the oil, salt, and pepper. Add the shrimp and toss to coat.

5   Brush the cooking grate clean. Drain and add the wood chips to the charcoal and put the lid on the grill. When the wood begins to smoke, spread the shrimp in a single layer on the grill pan and cook over DIRECT MEDIUM HEAT, with the lid closed as much as possible, until firm to the touch and just turning opaque in the center, 4 to 6 minutes, turning once. Transfer to a serving platter. Warm the tortillas over DIRECT MEDIUM HEAT for about 15 seconds on each side. Fill each tortilla with some of the lettuce mixture, a few shrimp, and a drizzle of the crema. Serve right away, with lime wedges and pickled jalapeño rings, if desired.

In some cases tortillas soften quickly when moistened by the shrimp and crema. If that happens, stack two tortillas together to make a double-thick wrap for the filling.

SHRIMP AND RICE SAUSAGES

WITH VIETNAMESE DIPPING SAUCE

IDEAL
GRILL:

SMOKE INTENSITY: moderate

PREP TIME: 1 hour

COOKING TIME: 6 to 8 minutes

SPECIAL EQUIPMENT:
perforated grill pan

SERVES: 4 to 6; 8 to 12 as an appetizer

Canola oil
1 tablespoon fish sauce
2 teaspoons granulated sugar
¼ cup minced scallions (white and light
   green parts only)
1½ teaspoons baking powder
½ teaspoon ground black pepper
2 pounds medium shrimp (31/35 count),
   peeled and deveined, tails removed
1 cup cooked short-grain rice,
   at room temperature

SAUCE
¼ cup fish sauce
¼ cup fresh lime juice
¼ cup granulated sugar
2 teaspoons seeded, minced Thai
   chile pepper
½ teaspoon minced garlic

2 large handfuls apple wood chips,
   soaked in water for at least 30 minutes

2 heads Boston lettuce, about 1 pound
   total, separated into leaves
   Fresh mint leaves
2 large carrots, peeled and shredded
1 English cucumber, cut in half lengthwise, thinly sliced into half-moons

You can use a food processor, but it's best to chop the shrimp with a knife for better texture.

1 In a large bowl whisk 1 tablespoon oil, the fish sauce, and sugar until the sugar dissolves. Stir in the scallions, baking powder, and pepper (the mixture will foam slightly). Chop the shrimp into a chunky paste. Add the shrimp and rice to the scallion mixture and mix thoroughly. Working with 2 tablespoons at a time, shape the mixture into 24 to 30 two-inch long sausages and place on an oiled sheet pan. Brush the top of each sausage with oil.

2 In a small, nonreactive bowl whisk the sauce ingredients until the sugar is dissolved.

3 Prepare a two-zone fire for low heat (250° to 350°F) (see pages 18–19) and preheat the grill pan on the cooking grate over direct heat.

4 Brush the cooking grate clean. Drain and add the wood chips to the charcoal and put the lid on the grill. When the wood begins to smoke, close the bottom vent on the grill and leave the top vent half open. Place the sausages in a single layer on the grill pan and cook over DIRECT LOW HEAT, with the lid closed as much as possible, until the sausages are plump, opaque, and golden, 6 to 8 minutes, turning once. Remove from the grill.

5 Place each sausage on a lettuce leaf and top with mint, carrots, and cucumber. Drizzle with the sauce or use sauce for dipping. Serve warm or at room temperature.

WARM SALAD OF SMOKED MACKEREL
AND ORANGE SUPREMES

IDEAL
GRILL:

SMOKE INTENSITY: moderate

PREP TIME: 45 minutes

COOKING TIME: 10 to 12 minutes

SERVES: 4

Cook the mackerel at the lower end of the medium heat range, around 350°F, to allow extra time for the smoke to penetrate the flesh.

3 large navel oranges

6 Atlantic mackerel fillets, each 4 to 5 ounces
  Kosher salt
  Ground black pepper
2 large handfuls hickory wood chips, soaked in water for at least 30 minutes

1 tablespoon cider vinegar
1 teaspoon Dijon mustard
1 teaspoon honey
3 tablespoons extra-virgin olive oil
6 ounces mixed baby greens
12 small pickled onions (from a jar)

1 Prepare a two-zone fire for medium heat (350° to 450°F) (see pages 18–19).

2 Supreme the oranges: Cut off a small slice from the top and bottom of each orange so the round fruit can stand upright. Use a serrated knife to cut the rind off the flesh in long arcs, starting at the top and following down along the natural curve of the fruit. Cut far enough into the flesh to remove the white pith but not so far as to damage the pulp. Then hold the peeled fruit in your hand and use a paring knife to cut between the flesh and the white membranes separating the individual segments. Allow the segments to fall into a bowl.

3 Season the mackerel fillets evenly with ¼ teaspoon salt and ¼ teaspoon pepper. Brush the cooking grate clean. Drain and add the wood chips to the charcoal and put the lid on the grill. When the wood begins to smoke, cook the fillets, skin side down, over INDIRECT MEDIUM HEAT, with the lid closed as much as possible, until the mackerel just barely begins to flake when you poke it with the tip of a knife, 10 to 12 minutes (do not turn). Transfer to a cutting board, let cool for a few minutes, and then peel off the skin. Chop the mackerel into bite-sized chunks.

4 In a large bowl whisk the vinegar, mustard, honey, ¼ teaspoon salt, and ¼ teaspoon pepper. Gradually whisk in the oil until the dressing is emulsified. Add the salad greens and toss to coat. Divide evenly among four serving plates. Top each plate with equal amounts of the orange supremes, mackerel, and onions.

SMOKED CATFISH FILLETS
WITH PECAN BROWN BUTTER

IDEAL GRILL:

SMOKE INTENSITY: moderate

PREP TIME: 20 minutes

COOKING TIME: about 12 minutes

SERVES: 6

PASTE
- 2 garlic cloves
- ½ teaspoon kosher salt
- 2 tablespoons extra-virgin olive oil
- 1 tablespoon paprika
- 2 teaspoons finely chopped fresh thyme leaves
- 1 teaspoon celery seed
- ½ teaspoon ground white pepper
- ⅛ teaspoon ground cayenne pepper

- 6 catfish fillets, each about 7 ounces and ½ inch thick

BUTTER
- 6 tablespoons (¾ stick) unsalted butter
- ½ cup coarsely chopped pecans
- 1 tablespoon fresh lemon juice
- 1 tablespoon chopped fresh Italian parsley leaves
- ¼ teaspoon kosher salt
- ⅛ teaspoon ground black pepper

- 1 large handful pecan wood chips, soaked in water for at least 30 minutes

Catfish fillets range in size. If your fillets are larger than seven ounces, just add a few more minutes of cooking time and cook until the fish is opaque when flaked with the tip of a knife.

1 Finely chop the garlic and then sprinkle with the salt. Use the side of a knife to smash the garlic into a paste. Keep swishing the knife back and forth until the garlic is so thin it's almost transparent. Transfer to a small bowl. Add the remaining paste ingredients and mix to combine thoroughly. Spread the paste on both sides of the catfish fillets. Allow the catfish to stand at room temperature for about 20 minutes while you preheat the grill.

2 Prepare a two-zone fire for medium heat (350° to 450°F) (see pages 18–19).

3 In a medium skillet over medium heat, melt the butter and cook just until it turns light brown, about 3 minutes. Remove from the heat. Stir in the remaining butter ingredients.

4 Brush the cooking grate clean. Drain and add the wood chips to the charcoal and put the lid on the grill. When the wood begins to smoke, cook the catfish over DIRECT MEDIUM HEAT, with the lid closed as much as possible, until the fish just barely begins to flake when you poke it with the tip of a knife, about 12 minutes, carefully turning once. Remove from the grill. Serve warm with the butter spooned over the top.

PROVENÇAL SALMON FILLETS
WITH SMOKED TOMATOES AND FENNEL

IDEAL GRILL:

SMOKE INTENSITY: mild

PREP TIME: 20 minutes

COOKING TIME: 22 to 28 minutes

SPECIAL EQUIPMENT:
8 metal or bamboo skewers (if using bamboo, soak in water for at least 30 minutes); spice mill

SERVES: 4

---

1 fennel bulb, about 1 pound, root end and stalks removed

12 ounces cherry tomatoes
Extra-virgin olive oil
Kosher salt
Ground black pepper

2 large handfuls hickory wood chips, soaked in water for at least 30 minutes

RUB

2 teaspoons fennel seed
1 teaspoon herbes de Provence
¼ teaspoon ground cayenne pepper

4 salmon fillets (with skin), each 6 to 8 ounces and about 1 inch thick, pin bones removed

---

Fennel bulbs separate nicely into layers (similar to onions) and so are perfect for skewering and then smoking over a smoldering fire.

1 Prepare the grill for direct cooking over medium heat (350° to 450°F) (see pages 22-23).

2 Cut the fennel bulb in half lengthwise and remove the thick, triangular core. Cut the halves into chunks about three layers thick and about as big as the tomatoes. Thread the fennel and tomatoes on separate skewers, brush them with oil, and season with salt and pepper.

3 Brush the cooking grates clean. Drain and add one handful of the wood chips to the smoker box of a gas grill, following manufacturer's instructions, and close the lid. When smoke appears, cook the fennel skewers over DIRECT MEDIUM HEAT, with the lid closed, for 6 to 8 minutes. Add the tomato skewers and continue cooking with the fennel over DIRECT MEDIUM HEAT, with the lid closed as much as possible, until the vegetables are tender and the fennel is lightly browned, 8 to 9 minutes more, turning once or twice. Remove from the grill as they are done. Increase the temperature of the grill to high heat (450° to 550°F).

4 In a spice mill crush the fennel seed. Pour into a small bowl and mix with the remaining rub ingredients, including 1 teaspoon salt and ½ teaspoon black pepper. Lightly brush the salmon fillets with oil and season evenly with the rub.

5 Brush the cooking grates clean. Drain and add the remaining wood chips to the smoker box and close the lid. When smoke appears, grill the salmon, flesh side down first, over DIRECT HIGH HEAT, with the lid closed, until you can lift the fillets off the cooking grate with tongs without sticking, 6 to 8 minutes. Turn the fillets over and continue cooking to your desired doneness, 2 to 3 minutes for medium rare. Remove from the grill and serve warm with the fennel and tomato skewers.

CEDAR-PLANKED SALMON
WITH APPLE-TARRAGON SALAD

IDEAL GRILL:

SMOKE INTENSITY: moderate

PREP TIME: 30 minutes

COOKING TIME: 15 to 20 minutes

SPECIAL EQUIPMENT: 1 untreated cedar plank, 12 to 15 inches long and about 7 inches wide and ½ to ¾ inch thick, soaked in water for at least 1 hour

SERVES: 4

SALAD
- 2 tablespoons sour cream
- 2 tablespoons fresh lemon juice
- ¼ teaspoon granulated sugar
- 2 Granny Smith apples, about 12 ounces total, cut into ¼-inch dice
- 1 tablespoon minced fresh tarragon leaves
  Kosher salt
  Ground black pepper

GLAZE
- ⅔ cup unsweetened apple juice
- 1 tablespoon whole-grain mustard

RUB
- 1 teaspoon kosher salt
- ½ teaspoon ground black pepper
- ½ teaspoon granulated sugar

- 1 salmon fillet (with skin), about 1½ pounds, pin bones removed
- 2 tablespoons minced fresh tarragon leaves
- 1 tablespoon minced scallion (white and light green parts only)

1 In a medium, nonreactive bowl whisk the sour cream, lemon juice, and sugar. Add the apples and tarragon and toss to coat. Season with salt and pepper. Cover and refrigerate until ready to serve.

2 In a small saucepan over high heat, boil the apple juice until it is reduced to 3 tablespoons, 12 to 15 minutes. Remove from the heat and stir in the mustard. Pour the glaze into a small bowl and let cool.

3 Prepare a two-zone fire for medium heat (350° to 450°F) (see pages 18–19).

4 In a small bowl combine the rub ingredients. Cut the salmon fillet in half lengthwise and then crosswise to make four individual portions, cutting right down to the skin but not through it. Season the flesh side of the fillet evenly with the tarragon and scallion and then the rub.

5 Brush the cooking grate clean. Place the soaked plank on the cooking grate over DIRECT MEDIUM HEAT and close the lid. After 5 to 10 minutes, when the plank begins to smoke and char, turn the plank over. Place the fillet on the plank and cook over DIRECT MEDIUM HEAT, with the lid closed, until lightly browned on the surface and cooked to your desired doneness, 15 to 20 minutes for medium rare, brushing with the glaze after the first 10 minutes of cooking time. (The cooking time will vary according to the thickness of the fillet.) Using sturdy tongs, carefully transfer the fillet on the plank to a heatproof surface.

6 Slide a spatula between the skin and flesh and transfer individual portions of the salmon to serving plates. Serve warm or at room temperature with the salad.

If at any point you see a lot of smoke pouring out of the grill, move the plank temporarily over indirect heat.

JUNIPER-LACED HOT-SMOKED SALMON

IDEAL GRILL:

SMOKE INTENSITY: strong

PREP TIME: 15 minutes

REFRIGERATION TIME: 4½ hours

STANDING TIME: 30 minutes, or for delayed smoking, 8 to 12 hours

COOKING TIME: about 2½ hours

SPECIAL EQUIPMENT:
mortar and pestle, electric fan

SERVES: 8

Some fillets look completely boneless, but if you run a fingertip over their surface you might feel the ends of tiny bones, called pin bones, which must be removed. Use needle-nose pliers or tweezers to grab the end of each bone and carefully pull it out at an angle.

½ cup gin
1 salmon fillet (with skin), about 3 pounds, pin bones removed
4 tablespoons juniper berries, divided
2 teaspoons black peppercorns
1 cup packed light brown sugar
½ cup kosher salt
1 tablespoon vegetable oil

3 fist-sized maple wood chunks

1 Pour the gin into a 15-by-10-inch glass or ceramic baking dish. Place the salmon fillet in the dish, skin side up, and spoon the gin all over the fillet. Cover and refrigerate for 30 minutes.

2 Using a mortar and pestle coarsely grind 2 tablespoons of the juniper berries and the peppercorns (or crush under a heavy saucepan on a cutting board). Pour the mixture into a medium bowl and combine with the brown sugar and salt. Remove the salmon from the dish and pat dry with paper towels. Discard the gin. Wash and dry the dish. Put about one-third of the brown sugar mixture in the dish. Place the salmon, skin side down, in the dish. Spread and pat the remaining brown sugar mixture over the flesh, covering it entirely. Cover and refrigerate for 4 hours.

3 Prepare the smoker for indirect cooking with very low heat (200° to 250°F) (see pages 20–21).

4 In a small bowl soak the remaining 2 tablespoons juniper berries in water while cooking the salmon.

5 Remove the salmon from the dish. Rinse under cold running water to remove the brown sugar mixture. Pat dry with paper towels. Brush the salmon skin with the oil. Place the salmon on a large wire rack set over a large, rimmed sheet pan. Let stand at room temperature with a table fan trained on the salmon until the surface looks lightly glazed and feels tacky, about 30 minutes. (Or refrigerate the salmon on the rack setup, uncovered, for 8 to 12 hours.)

6 Brush the cooking grate clean. Add one wood chunk to the charcoal. Smoke the salmon fillet, skin side down, over **INDIRECT VERY LOW HEAT**, with the lid closed, until the salmon is firm and has a golden, almost deep brown patina, about 2½ hours. Add more lit briquettes as necessary to maintain the heat. Every 45 minutes, add one more wood chunk to the charcoal. During the last 15 minutes of cooking time, drain and add the juniper berries to the charcoal. Remove the salmon from the smoker and let rest for about 5 minutes. Serve warm.

Once smoked, the salmon can be wrapped in plastic wrap and frozen for up to four months.

DIJON SALMON STRIPS
ON ORANGE CARPACCIO

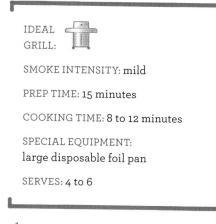

IDEAL GRILL:

SMOKE INTENSITY: mild

PREP TIME: 15 minutes

COOKING TIME: 8 to 12 minutes

SPECIAL EQUIPMENT:
large disposable foil pan

SERVES: 4 to 6

For the best taste possible, use wild salmon.

GLAZE
- 1 tablespoon whole-grain Dijon mustard
- 1 tablespoon mayonnaise
- 2 teaspoons mustard seed
- 2 teaspoons packed light brown sugar
- ⅛ teaspoon ground cayenne pepper

- Extra-virgin olive oil
- 1 large skinless salmon fillet, about 1½ pounds and ¾ to 1 inch thick, pin bones removed
- ¼ teaspoon kosher salt
- ⅛ teaspoon ground black pepper

- 3 large navel oranges

- 2 large handfuls apple wood chips, soaked in water for at least 30 minutes
- 1 tablespoon roughly chopped fresh basil leaves
- ¼ teaspoon crushed red pepper flakes

1 In a small bowl mix the glaze ingredients.

2 Lightly coat the bottom of a large disposable foil pan with oil. Cut the fillet crosswise into 8 to 10 equal pieces and transfer them to the pan, flesh side up. Season the top of the salmon fillets evenly with the salt and pepper and then spread on the glaze. Cover the pan and refrigerate until ready to cook.

3 Prepare the grill for indirect cooking over medium heat (350° to 450°F) (see pages 22–23).

4 Cut off a small slice from the top and bottom of each orange so the round fruit can stand upright. Use a serrated knife to cut the rind off the flesh in long arcs, starting at the top and following down along the natural curve of the fruit. Cut far enough into the flesh to remove the white pith but not so far as to damage the pulp. Cut each orange crosswise into ⅛-inch slices. Arrange the orange slices on the bottom of a serving platter. Drizzle about 1 teaspoon oil over the orange slices.

5 Brush the cooking grates clean. Drain and add the wood chips to the smoker box of a gas grill, following manufacturer's instructions, and close the lid. When smoke is pouring out of the grill, set the pan with the salmon over INDIRECT MEDIUM HEAT, close the lid, and cook to your desired doneness, 8 to 12 minutes for medium rare (do not turn). Remove from the grill and arrange the salmon pieces on top of the orange slices. Garnish with the basil and red pepper flakes. Serve warm.

TERIYAKI TUNA AND PINEAPPLE KABOBS

IDEAL GRILL:

SMOKE INTENSITY: moderate

PREP TIME: 30 minutes

MARINATING TIME: 1 hour

COOKING TIME: 6 to 8 minutes

SPECIAL EQUIPMENT: 4 to 6 metal or bamboo skewers (if using bamboo, soak in water for at least 30 minutes)

SERVES: 4 to 6

MARINADE
- ½ cup pineapple juice, preferably refrigerated instead of canned
- ½ cup soy sauce
- ¼ cup packed light brown sugar
- 2 tablespoons thinly sliced dark green scallion tops
- 1 tablespoon grated fresh ginger
- 2 teaspoons minced garlic

- 2 pounds tuna fillets, cut into 1½-inch cubes

- 2 red bell peppers, cut into 1½-inch pieces
- 6 large scallions (white and light green parts only), cut into 1½-inch pieces
- 8 ounces fresh pineapple, cut into 1½-inch chunks
  Extra-virgin olive oil

- 2 large handfuls apple wood chips, soaked in water for at least 30 minutes

When making kabobs, it's important that all pieces of food are about the same size to promote even cooking.

1 In a large, nonreactive bowl whisk the marinade ingredients until the sugar dissolves. Add the tuna and gently turn to coat. Cover and refrigerate for 1 hour, turning occasionally.

2 Prepare a two-zone fire for medium heat (350° to 450°F) (see pages 18–19).

3 Thread the peppers, scallions, and pineapple alternately onto skewers, leaving a little room between each piece. Thread the tuna on separate skewers. Lightly brush the vegetables and the tuna with oil.

4 Brush the cooking grate clean. Drain and add the wood chips to the charcoal and put the lid on the grill. When the wood begins to smoke, cook the kabobs over DIRECT MEDIUM HEAT, with the lid closed as much as possible, until the vegetables are crisp-tender, the pineapple is lightly browned, and the tuna is just pink at the center, 6 to 8 minutes, turning once or twice. Remove from the grill and serve right away.

CEDAR-PLANKED TUNA SALAD

WITH HONEY-DIJON DRESSING AND CRISPY PECANS

IDEAL GRILL:

SMOKE INTENSITY: mild

PREP TIME: 15 minutes

COOKING TIME: 22 to 31 minutes

SPECIAL EQUIPMENT:
perforated grill pan; 1 untreated cedar plank, 12 to 15 inches long and about 7 inches wide and ½ to ¾ inch thick, soaked in water for at least 1 hour

SERVES: 4 to 6

Cedar planks come in different thicknesses. For this recipe, the plank was about one-half inch thick, but if you use a thinner one, the cooking time will be shorter.

DRESSING
- 3 tablespoons honey
- 3 tablespoons Dijon mustard
- 2 tablespoons white wine vinegar
- ¼ cup extra-virgin olive oil
  Kosher salt

- ½ cup pecan halves
- 8 ounces sugar snap peas (about 2 cups)
- 6–8 scallions (white and light green parts only), cut into ½-inch pieces
  Extra-virgin olive oil
  Ground black pepper

- 2 tuna steaks, each about 1 pound and 1 inch thick
- 1 teaspoon paprika
- 1 tablespoon finely chopped fresh dill
- 6 ounces mixed baby greens

1 In a small, nonreactive bowl whisk the honey, mustard, and vinegar. Slowly drizzle in the oil, whisking until the dressing is emulsified. Season with ½ teaspoon salt and set aside.

2 Prepare the grill for direct cooking over medium heat (350° to 450°F) (see pages 22–23) and preheat the grill pan on the cooking grates.

3 Spread the pecans in a single layer on the grill pan. Cook over DIRECT MEDIUM HEAT, with the lid closed as much as possible, until they darken a shade and are fragrant, 5 to 10 minutes, stirring once or twice. Wearing insulated barbecue mitts, carefully pour the nuts from the grill pan into a small bowl to cool (they will crisp as they cool) and place the grill pan back over direct heat.

4 In a large bowl toss the sugar snap peas and scallions with oil and season with salt and pepper. Arrange the vegetables in a single layer on the grill pan. Cook over DIRECT MEDIUM HEAT, with the lid closed as much as possible, until the vegetables are slightly softened and charred, 5 to 6 minutes, stirring occasionally. Wearing insulated barbecue mitts, remove the pan from the grill and transfer the vegetables to a salad bowl.

5 Season the tuna steaks evenly with the paprika, dill, and salt and pepper. Place the soaked plank over DIRECT MEDIUM HEAT and close the lid. After 5 to 10 minutes, when the plank begins to smoke and char, turn the plank over. Place the tuna on the plank and cook over DIRECT MEDIUM HEAT, with the lid closed, until the tuna is a little pink in the center and is beginning to flake, 12 to 15 minutes. Remove from the grill and cut into bite-sized pieces.

6 Put the mixed greens, pecans, and tuna in the salad bowl with the vegetables. Pour the dressing over the salad, toss to mix, and serve immediately.

WOOD-GRILLED TUNA STEAKS
WITH SMOKED FENNEL RELISH

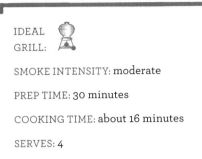

IDEAL
GRILL:

SMOKE INTENSITY: moderate

PREP TIME: 30 minutes

COOKING TIME: about 16 minutes

SERVES: 4

---

1 fennel bulb, about 1 pound
1 large red bell pepper
4 ripe plum tomatoes, halved lengthwise
   Extra-virgin olive oil

2 large handfuls oak wood chips,
   soaked in water for at least 30 minutes

2 tablespoons sherry vinegar
½ teaspoon smoked paprika
1 teaspoon kosher salt, divided
¾ teaspoon ground black pepper, divided
⅓ cup hazelnuts, toasted, skinned,
   and coarsely chopped
½ cup chopped fresh Italian
   parsley leaves

4 tuna steaks, each about 6 ounces and
   1 inch thick

To toast the hazelnuts, spread them on a baking sheet and bake in a preheated 350°F oven until the skins are cracked and the nut flesh is toasted, about 10 minutes, turning occasionally. Transfer to a clean kitchen towel and let cool for 5 minutes. Wrap the hazelnuts in the towel and rub them against each other to remove most of their papery skins. Don't worry if every last bit of skin doesn't come off.

1 Prepare a two-zone fire for high heat (450° to 550°F) (see pages 18–19).

2 Cut off the thick stalks and the root end from the fennel bulb and discard. Cut the bulb in half lengthwise and then cut away and remove the thick, triangular core. Cut the fennel vertically into ½-inch slices. Cut off the top and bottom of the bell pepper. Make a cut down the side and open it up into a large strip. Remove the ribs and seeds. Brush the fennel slices and tomato halves with 1 tablespoon of oil.

3 Brush the cooking grate clean. Drain and add half of the wood chips to the charcoal and put the lid on the grill. When the wood begins to smoke, cook the fennel, pepper (shiny skin side down), and tomato halves (cut side down) over DIRECT HIGH HEAT, with the lid closed as much as possible. Cook the fennel until it is crisp-tender, about 8 minutes, turning once; the bell pepper until it is blackened and blistered, 6 to 8 minutes (do not turn); and the tomatoes until they are charred, about 6 minutes, turning once. Remove from the grill as they are done. Place the pepper strip in a bowl, cover with plastic wrap to trap the steam, and let stand for 5 to 10 minutes. Decrease the temperature of the grill to medium heat (350° to 450°F).

4 Remove the pepper from the bowl and peel away and discard the charred skin. Cut the fennel, pepper, and tomatoes into ½-inch dice.

5 In a medium, nonreactive bowl whisk the vinegar, paprika, ½ teaspoon of the salt, and ½ teaspoon of the pepper. Gradually whisk in ¼ cup of oil. Add the fennel, pepper, tomatoes, hazelnuts, and parsley to the bowl and mix. Set aside at room temperature.

6 Brush the tuna steaks on both sides with oil and season evenly with the remaining ½ teaspoon salt and the remaining ¼ teaspoon pepper. Brush the cooking grate clean. Drain and add the remaining wood chips to the charcoal and put the lid on the grill. When the wood begins to smoke, cook the tuna over DIRECT MEDIUM HEAT, with the lid closed as much as possible, until just turning opaque throughout, about 8 minutes, turning once. Remove from the grill and serve warm with the relish.

LEMON-GARLIC SWORDFISH STEAKS
WITH SMOKED PEPPERS AND ONIONS

IDEAL GRILL:

SMOKE INTENSITY: mild

PREP TIME: 20 minutes

MARINATING TIME: 1 to 2 hours

COOKING TIME: 18 to 22 minutes

SPECIAL EQUIPMENT:
perforated grill pan

SERVES: 4

MARINADE
- ¼ cup extra-virgin olive oil
- 1 tablespoon grated lemon zest
- 3 tablespoons fresh lemon juice
- 1 tablespoon minced garlic
- 1 teaspoon kosher salt
- ½ teaspoon dried thyme

- 4 swordfish steaks, each 8 to 10 ounces and about 1 inch thick

- 2 red bell peppers, cut into ¼-inch slices
- 1 medium yellow onion, halved and cut into ¼-inch slices
- 1 tablespoon extra-virgin olive oil
- ½ teaspoon kosher salt
- ¼ teaspoon ground black pepper

- 1 large handful mesquite wood chips, soaked in water for at least 30 minutes

- 1 tablespoon cider vinegar
- ½ cup pitted kalamata olives, each cut in half

Take care not to overcook the fish, which should be moist and just beginning to flake when removed from the grill.

1 In a small bowl whisk the marinade ingredients.

2 Place the swordfish steaks in a shallow glass or ceramic dish large enough to hold them in a single layer. Pour in the marinade, turning the swordfish to coat evenly. Cover with plastic wrap and refrigerate for 1 to 2 hours.

3 Prepare the grill for direct cooking over low heat (250° to 350°F) (see pages 22–23) and preheat the grill pan on the cooking grates.

4 In a medium bowl combine the pepper and onion slices with the oil, salt, and pepper; carefully turn to coat.

5 Drain and add the wood chips to the smoker box of a gas grill, following manufacturer's instructions, and close the lid. When the wood begins to smoke, arrange the vegetables in a single layer on the grill pan and cook over DIRECT LOW HEAT, with the lid closed as much as possible, until slightly charred and softened, 10 to 12 minutes, turning occasionally. Wearing insulated barbecue mitts, remove the pan from the grill and transfer the vegetables to a small, nonreactive bowl. Stir in the vinegar and olives and set aside.

6 Increase the temperature of the grill to high heat (450° to 550°F).

7 Brush the cooking grates clean. Lift the swordfish from the dish and let the excess marinade drip back into the dish. Discard the marinade. Cook the swordfish over DIRECT HIGH HEAT, with the lid closed as much as possible, until just opaque in the center but still juicy, 8 to 10 minutes, turning once. Transfer to individual plates or a serving platter and spoon the pepper and onion slices around the swordfish. Serve warm.

PROSCIUTTO-WRAPPED TROUT

WITH SPINACH-PINE NUT STUFFING

STUFFING

  1 tablespoon extra-virgin olive oil
  2 tablespoons minced shallot
 10 ounces fresh baby spinach
  1 cup fresh bread crumbs
  3 tablespoons chopped golden raisins
  2 tablespoons pine nuts, toasted
  2 tablespoons finely grated
     Parmigiano-Reggiano® cheese
  1 teaspoon minced fresh
     rosemary leaves
  2 tablespoons dry white wine *or*
     dry vermouth
     Kosher salt
     Ground black pepper

  4 whole trout, each 12 to 14 ounces,
     butterflied and deboned
 16 thin prosciutto slices, about
     8 ounces total

  1 large handful maple or oak wood
     chips, soaked in water for at least
     30 minutes
  1 lemon, quartered (optional)

To toast the pine nuts, spread them in a medium skillet over medium heat, and cook until lightly browned, about 2 minutes, stirring occasionally. Transfer to a plate to cool.

1 Prepare a two-zone fire for medium heat (350° to 450°F) (see pages 18–19).

2 In a large skillet over medium heat, heat the oil. Add the shallot and cook until softened, about 3 minutes, stirring occasionally. Add the spinach and cover. Cook until the spinach is wilted and tender, about 5 minutes, stirring occasionally. Remove from the heat and let cool.

3 Roughly chop the spinach and place the chopped spinach with the shallot in a medium bowl. Mix in the bread crumbs, raisins, pine nuts, cheese, and rosemary. Stir in the wine. Season with salt and pepper. Divide the spinach mixture among the trout, packing it evenly into the body cavities. Close the trout over the filling.

4 Overlap four pieces of prosciutto. Place a trout vertically along one short side of the prosciutto bed. Roll the trout with the prosciutto, wrapping it up. Set aside and repeat with the remaining trout.

5 Brush the cooking grate clean. Drain and add the wood chips to the charcoal and put the lid on the grill. When the wood begins to smoke, cook the trout, with the seam side of the prosciutto down first, over DIRECT MEDIUM HEAT, with the lid closed as much as possible, until the prosciutto is crisp and the trout is cooked through, 12 to 16 minutes, turning once. Remove from the grill and serve right away with lemon quarters, if desired.

SMOKED HERRING AND ONIONS

IDEAL GRILL:

SMOKE INTENSITY: moderate

PREP TIME: 20 minutes

COOKING TIME: 5 to 12 minutes

SERVES: 4

8   Atlantic herring, each about
    5 ounces, cleaned
2   large yellow onions, cut crosswise
    into ⅓-inch slices
    Vegetable oil

2   large handfuls apple wood chips,
    soaked in water for at least 30 minutes

4   slices pumpernickel bread
    Whole-grain Dijon mustard
    Sour cream
    Fresh Italian parsley leaves

The fish are butterflied, not filleted, which is an important distinction. They have two flaps of fillets attached at the bottom by the tail. If filleted into two fillets, they will cook too quickly.

1   Prepare a two-zone fire for medium heat (350° to 450°F) (see pages 18–19).

2   Butterfly the herring and remove the heads and central bones. Leave the tails attached. Lightly brush the herring and onion slices on both sides with oil.

3   Brush the cooking grate clean. Drain and add the wood chips to the charcoal and put the lid on the grill. When the wood begins to smoke, cook the herring, skin side down, over INDIRECT MEDIUM HEAT, with the lid closed, until cooked through, 5 to 10 minutes depending on the thickness of the fillets (do not turn). At the same time, cook the onion slices over DIRECT MEDIUM HEAT until tender and nicely browned, 8 to 12 minutes, turning once or twice. Remove from the grill as they are done.

4   Serve the herring and onions on pumpernickel bread slices with mustard and sour cream to spread on the bread as desired. Top with parsley.

ROSEMARY-SMOKED WHOLE BRANZINO

WITH GREEK COUNTRY SALAD

IDEAL
GRILL:

SMOKE INTENSITY: moderate

PREP TIME: 30 minutes

STANDING TIME: 30 minutes to 2 hours

COOKING TIME: about 15 minutes

SPECIAL EQUIPMENT: butcher's twine

SERVES: 4

The easiest way to tell if fish is fresh at the market is to ask to smell it. It should smell like the ocean at high tide on a spring morning. If the branzino is not at its prime, consider any other whole sea fish that weighs around 1¼ pounds, such as snapper, striped bass, sea bass, or mullet.

2   whole branzino, each about 1¼ pounds, cleaned, gutted, scaled, gills and all fins removed
3   medium lemons
2   tablespoons extra-virgin olive oil
     Kosher salt
     Ground black pepper
10 fresh rosemary sprigs, each about 6 inches long

SALAD
¼   cup extra-virgin olive oil
2   ripe plum tomatoes, seeded and diced
1   English cucumber, diced
1   small green bell pepper, diced
¼   cup minced red onion
20 pitted kalamata olives, roughly chopped

1 Cut three or four parallel slashes about ½ inch deep and 1 inch apart on each side of the branzino. Cut one of the lemons in half crosswise. Squeeze 2 tablespoons of juice into a medium, nonreactive bowl and set aside for the salad. Cut the other two lemons into thin slices. Set aside the slices of one lemon to serve with the smoked branzino. The slices of the other lemon will be used inside the branzino.

2 Lightly brush each branzino with the oil and season evenly, inside and outside, with salt and pepper. Place half the lemon slices from one lemon, and one rosemary sprig, cut in half, inside the cavity of each branzino. Tie each branzino crosswise with butcher's twine in two or three places to hold it closed. Refrigerate the branzino while you preheat the grill. Soak the remaining eight rosemary sprigs in water for at least 30 minutes.

3 Pour ¼ cup oil into the medium bowl with the reserved lemon juice and whisk to combine. Add the remaining salad ingredients and mix well. Season with salt and pepper. Let stand at room temperature for at least 30 minutes. If desired, to fully incorporate the flavors, let the salad sit at room temperature for up to 2 hours.

4 Prepare a two-zone fire for medium heat (350° to 450°F) (see pages 18–19).

5 Brush the cooking grate clean. Drain and add the rosemary sprigs to the charcoal and put the lid on the grill. When the sprigs begin to smoke, cook the branzino over DIRECT MEDIUM HEAT, with the lid closed as much as possible, until the flesh is opaque near the bone but still juicy, about 15 minutes, using a metal spatula to carefully turn once (do not be concerned if the skin sticks to the cooking grate). Remove from the grill.

6 Carefully remove the twine from the fish and then cut off the heads and tails. Cut along the backbone and then open the fish like a book. Remove the bones, and lift the flesh off the skin. Serve alongside the salad with the lemon slices.

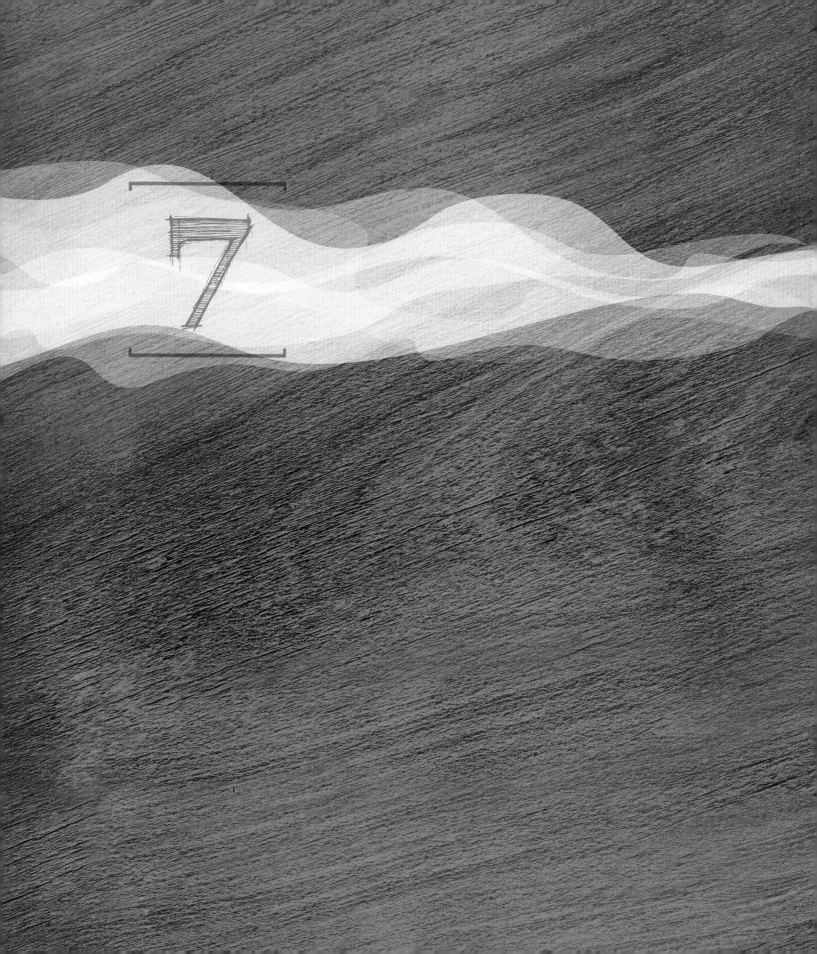

Vegetables and Sides

GRILL-ROASTED ARTICHOKES
WITH SMOKED GARLIC AIOLI

IDEAL
GRILL:

SMOKE INTENSITY: moderate

PREP TIME: 30 minutes

COOKING TIME: about 47 minutes

SERVES: 6

Choose artichokes that are compact and heavy for their size, and that squeak when their leaves are squeezed together.

1 lemon
6 artichokes, each 7 to 8 ounces
2 medium garlic heads
2 tablespoons plus 1 teaspoon
  extra-virgin olive oil, divided
1 teaspoon water
  Kosher salt
  Ground black pepper

2 large handfuls oak wood chips,
  soaked in water for at least 30 minutes

1 cup mayonnaise
2 tablespoons chopped fresh Italian
  parsley leaves

1 Prepare a two-zone fire for medium heat (350° to 450°F) (see pages 18–19).

2 Cut the lemon in half and squeeze the juice into a large, nonreactive bowl; fill the bowl two-thirds full with water. Reserve the lemon halves. Working with one artichoke at a time, trim the very end of the stem (if attached) and remove the smallest leaves. Using scissors, snip off the thorny tips from the outer leaves. As you work, rub the cut surfaces with the pulp side of the lemon halves. Put the trimmed artichokes in the lemon water.

3 Cut off the tops of the garlic heads to expose the cloves; discard the tops. Place the garlic heads side by side on a square of aluminum foil. Wrap the foil around the garlic, like a canoe, leaving the tops exposed. Drizzle with 1 teaspoon of the oil and 1 teaspoon water and season with a pinch of salt and pepper.

4 Drain the artichokes. Place each artichoke on a square of aluminum foil. Drizzle the remaining 2 tablespoons of oil over the artichokes and season them evenly with 1½ teaspoons salt and ¼ teaspoon pepper. Wrap each artichoke in its foil.

5 Brush the cooking grate clean. Drain and add one handful of the wood chips to the charcoal and put the lid on the grill. When the wood begins to smoke, cook the garlic and artichokes over **INDIRECT MEDIUM HEAT**, with the lid closed as much as possible, for about 40 minutes. Remove the garlic from the grill and let cool slightly.

6 Open the foil to expose the artichokes. Drain and add the second handful of wood chips to the charcoal. Continue grilling the artichokes until a large leaf can easily be pulled off, about 7 minutes more, turning the artichokes over once in the foil. Remove the artichokes from the grill.

7 Squeeze out the garlic cloves into a medium bowl. Mash the garlic with a fork. Add the mayonnaise and parsley and mix. Season with salt and pepper. Serve the artichokes warm or at room temperature with the aioli.

SUMMER VEGETABLE SUCCOTASH

3 medium zucchini, ends trimmed, each cut in half lengthwise

2 tablespoons extra-virgin olive oil, divided

2 ears fresh corn, husked

1 large red bell pepper

½ medium red onion, finely chopped

¾ teaspoon kosher salt, divided

2 teaspoons minced garlic

1 package (10 ounces) frozen lima beans, thawed

2 tablespoons finely chopped fresh oregano or basil leaves

¼ teaspoon ground black pepper

1 Prepare a two-zone fire for medium heat (350° to 450°F) (see pages 18–19).

2 Brush the cooking grate clean. Brush the zucchini with 1 tablespoon of the oil. Cook the zucchini, corn, and pepper over DIRECT MEDIUM HEAT, with the lid closed as much as possible, until the zucchini is crisp-tender, the corn is browned in spots and tender, and the pepper is blackened and blistered all over, turning occasionally. The zucchini will take about 6 minutes, and the corn and the pepper will take 10 to 12 minutes. Remove from the grill as they are done. Put the pepper in a bowl, cover with plastic wrap to trap the steam, and let stand for about 10 minutes.

3 When the vegetables are cool enough to handle, remove and discard the stem end, skin, and seeds from the pepper and cut the pepper and zucchini into ½-inch dice. Cut the kernels off the corn cobs.

4 In a large skillet over medium heat, warm the remaining 1 tablespoon oil. Add the onion and ¼ teaspoon of the salt and cook until tender, about 4 minutes, stirring occasionally. Stir in the garlic and cook until fragrant, about 1 minute. Add the lima beans, zucchini, corn, and pepper. Cover and cook until heated through, about 3 minutes, stirring occasionally. Stir in the oregano, the remaining ½ teaspoon salt, and the pepper. Serve right away.

Any kind of fresh summer bean can be used instead of the frozen lima beans. You will need about 1½ cups shelled beans. Cook in boiling water until just tender, about 5 minutes. Drain and rinse under cold running water.

ASPARAGUS AND PANCETTA
WITH LEMON-TARRAGON VINAIGRETTE

IDEAL GRILL:

SMOKE INTENSITY: mild

PREP TIME: 15 minutes

COOKING TIME: 6 to 8 minutes

SERVES: 4 to 6

Choose asparagus spears about as thick as your finger, as they fare better on the grill than pencil-thin spears.

3 ounces pancetta *or* 2 slices thick-cut bacon, diced
2 pounds asparagus
   Extra-virgin olive oil
   Kosher salt
   Ground black pepper

VINAIGRETTE
1 tablespoon finely grated lemon zest
2 tablespoons fresh lemon juice
2 tablespoons white wine vinegar
1 tablespoon finely diced shallot
2 teaspoons finely chopped fresh tarragon leaves
1 teaspoon honey

1 small handful hickory wood chips, soaked in water for at least 30 minutes

1 In a small skillet over medium heat, cook the diced pancetta until crisp and browned, 4 to 6 minutes, stirring occasionally. Drain on paper towels.

2 Prepare a two-zone fire for medium heat (350° to 450°F) (see pages 18–19).

3 Remove and discard the tough bottom of each asparagus spear by grasping at each end and bending it gently until the spear snaps at its natural point of tenderness, usually about two-thirds of the way down the spear. Drizzle the spears with oil and lightly season with salt and pepper.

4 In a small, nonreactive bowl whisk the vinaigrette ingredients. Slowly add ¼ cup of oil and whisk until the vinaigrette is emulsified. Season with salt and pepper.

5 Brush the cooking grate clean. Drain and add the wood chips to the charcoal and put the lid on the grill. When the wood begins to smoke, cook the asparagus over DIRECT MEDIUM HEAT, with the lid closed as much as possible, until tender, 6 to 8 minutes, turning occasionally.

6 Transfer the asparagus to a serving platter, drizzle with the vinaigrette, and top with the pancetta. Serve warm or at room temperature.

CHICKPEA AND MOZZARELLA SALAD
WITH SMOKED EGGPLANT AND TOMATOES

IDEAL GRILL:

SMOKE INTENSITY: mild

PREP TIME: 30 minutes

COOKING TIME: 15 to 20 minutes

COOLING TIME: about 30 minutes

MARINATING TIME: at least 1 hour

SERVES: 4 to 6

The chickpeas will absorb liquid and smoke from the eggplant and tomatoes while the salad marinates. Serve as a side dish or as a vegetarian main course.

VINAIGRETTE
2 teaspoons finely grated lime zest
¼ cup fresh lime juice
¼ cup extra-virgin olive oil
1 teaspoon minced garlic
½ teaspoon ground cumin
¼ teaspoon ground cayenne pepper

   Kosher salt
   Ground black pepper

4 medium plum tomatoes, each
   halved lengthwise
1 globe eggplant, about 1 pound, ends
   trimmed, halved lengthwise
3–4 scallions, ends trimmed

1 large handful mesquite wood chips,
   soaked in water for at least 30 minutes
2 cans (each 15 ounces)
   chickpeas, rinsed
1 large ball (8 ounces) fresh mozzarella
   cheese, cut into ¼-inch cubes
¼ cup roughly chopped fresh Italian
   parsley leaves

1 Prepare the grill for direct cooking over low heat (250° to 350°F) (see pages 22–23).

2 In a small, nonreactive bowl whisk the vinaigrette ingredients. Season with salt and pepper. Lightly brush the vegetables with some of the vinaigrette. Reserve the remaining vinaigrette.

3 Brush the cooking grates clean. Drain and add the wood chips to the smoker box of a gas grill, following manufacturer's instructions, and close the lid. When the wood begins to smoke, place the vegetables over DIRECT LOW HEAT, close the lid, and cook until the vegetables are tender and the tomato and eggplant skins wrinkle and start to brown, turning occasionally. The eggplant will take 15 to 20 minutes, the tomatoes will take 10 to 15 minutes, and the scallions will take about 10 minutes. Remove from the grill as they are done.

4 Place the tomatoes and eggplant in a large, nonreactive bowl and let cool for about 30 minutes (during this time, the tomatoes and eggplant will release some liquid). After the eggplant and tomatoes have cooled, transfer them to a cutting board; reserve the liquid. Cut all of the vegetables into bite-sized pieces. Put the vegetables back in the bowl with the liquid and add the chickpeas, cheese, and the reserved vinaigrette. Toss to coat. Set aside at room temperature for at least 1 hour, or in the refrigerator for up to 8 hours.

5 Before serving, mix in the parsley and season with salt and pepper. Served chilled or at room temperature.

VEGETABLE BULGUR SALAD
WITH FETA AND MINT

IDEAL GRILL:

SMOKE INTENSITY: mild

PREP TIME: 15 minutes, plus about 30 minutes to soak the bulgur

COOKING TIME: 12 to 15 minutes

STANDING TIME: at least 30 minutes

SERVES: 6 to 8

1½ cups bulgur
1½ cups boiling water

VINAIGRETTE
½ cup roughly chopped fresh mint leaves
3 tablespoons cider vinegar
2 teaspoons Dijon mustard
1 garlic clove, minced

Extra-virgin olive oil
Kosher salt
Ground black pepper

2 portabello mushrooms, each about 4 ounces, stems and gills removed
2 medium zucchini, about 12 ounces total, ends trimmed, each cut in half lengthwise
2 red bell peppers, about 12 ounces total, each cut into 4 planks

3 large handfuls apple wood chips, soaked in water for at least 30 minutes

12 ounces cherry tomatoes, each cut into quarters
4 ounces crumbled feta cheese
½ cup roughly chopped fresh Italian parsley leaves

1 In a large, nonreactive bowl mix the bulgur with the boiling water and let soak until the water is absorbed, about 30 minutes.

2 Prepare the grill for direct cooking over low heat (250° to 350°F) (see pages 22–23).

3 In a small bowl combine the vinaigrette ingredients. Whisk in ⅓ cup oil and season with 1 teaspoon salt and ½ teaspoon pepper. Pour the vinaigrette over the bulgur and toss to coat.

4 Lightly brush the mushrooms, zucchini, and peppers with oil and season evenly with salt and pepper.

5 Brush the cooking grates clean. Drain and add the wood chips to the smoker box of a gas grill, following manufacturer's instructions, and close the lid. When the wood begins to smoke, cook the vegetables over DIRECT LOW HEAT, with the lid closed as much as possible, until crisp-tender and lightly charred, 12 to 15 minutes, turning occasionally. Remove from the grill as they are done.

6 Cut the vegetables into ½-inch pieces and add to the bulgur. Gently fold in the tomatoes, cheese, and parsley. Set the salad aside at room temperature for at least 30 minutes, or cover and refrigerate for up to 24 hours. Serve at room temperature.

This salad is better the next day because the smokiness deepens as the ingredients mellow.

SMOKED ARTICHOKE PASTA
WITH LEMONY VINAIGRETTE

IDEAL GRILL:

SMOKE INTENSITY: mild

PREP TIME: 25 minutes

COOKING TIME: 10 to 12 minutes

SPECIAL EQUIPMENT:
perforated grill pan

SERVES: 6 to 8

DRESSING
¼ cup fresh lemon juice
¼ cup finely chopped kalamata olives
1 teaspoon finely chopped fresh thyme leaves
½ cup extra-virgin olive oil
Kosher salt
Ground black pepper

3 medium bell peppers, preferably 1 red, 1 yellow, and 1 orange, each cut into ¼-inch strips
2 cans (each 14 ounces) artichoke hearts (not in marinade) *or* 12 frozen artichoke hearts, thawed, drained, and quartered
¼ cup extra-virgin olive oil
2 teaspoons minced garlic

1 large handful hickory or oak wood chips, soaked in water for at least 30 minutes

8 ounces dried penne pasta
8 ounces fresh mozzarella cheese, cut into ¼-inch cubes

To achieve the best possible browning of the artichokes, drain off as much liquid as possible and coat them evenly with oil.

1 Prepare the grill for direct cooking over medium heat (350° to 450°F) (see pages 22–23) and preheat the grill pan on the cooking grates.

2 In a large, nonreactive serving bowl whisk the lemon juice, olives, and thyme. Slowly drizzle and whisk in ½ cup oil until it is emulsified. Season with salt and pepper. Set aside.

3 In a large bowl mix the peppers and artichokes with ¼ cup oil and the garlic.

4 Drain and add the wood chips to the smoker box of a gas grill, following manufacturer's instructions, and close the lid. When the wood begins to smoke, arrange the peppers and artichokes in a single layer on the grill pan. Cook over DIRECT MEDIUM HEAT, with the lid closed as much as possible, until slightly charred and softened, 10 to 12 minutes, turning occasionally. Wearing insulated barbecue mitts, remove the pan from the grill and set it on a heatproof surface. Transfer the vegetables to the large serving bowl with the dressing.

5 Cook the pasta in a large pot of boiling, salted water according to package directions. Drain the pasta and add to the serving bowl. Add the cheese and toss to combine. Serve warm or at room temperature.

SMOKED MARINATED TOFU
WITH ASIAN CABBAGE SLAW

IDEAL
GRILL:

SMOKE INTENSITY: strong

PREP TIME: 20 minutes

MARINATING TIME: 1 to 2 hours

COOKING TIME: about 2 hours

SERVES: 6

Do not use silken tofu or even firm tofu for this recipe. Only extra-firm tofu will be able to sit on the cooking grate for two hours without falling apart.

3 packages (each 14 to 16 ounces) extra-firm tofu, drained
6 tablespoons soy sauce, divided
6 tablespoons rice vinegar, divided
3 tablespoons fish sauce (not *patis*)

4 fist-sized hickory wood chunks

6 tablespoons canola oil, divided
2 teaspoons granulated sugar
1 teaspoon hot chili paste, such as *sambal oelek*
2 tablespoons toasted sesame oil
1 small head napa cabbage, about 2¼ pounds, cored and thinly sliced
2 medium bell peppers, 1 red and 1 yellow, julienned
4 medium scallions (white and light green parts only), thinly sliced
Kosher salt

1 Cut each tofu block in half horizontally to make six rectangular slabs. In a large glass or ceramic baking dish large enough to hold the tofu in a single layer, whisk 3 tablespoons of the soy sauce, 3 tablespoons of the vinegar, and the fish sauce. Add the tofu and turn to coat. Refrigerate for 1 to 2 hours, basting occasionally.

2 Prepare the smoker for indirect cooking with very low heat (200° to 250°F) (see pages 20–21). When the temperature reaches 225°F, add two wood chunks to the charcoal.

3 Remove the tofu from the marinade and pat dry with paper towels. Brush the tofu with 2 tablespoons of the canola oil. Brush the cooking grate clean. Smoke the tofu over INDIRECT VERY LOW HEAT, with the lid closed, until it is a light mahogany brown, about 2 hours. Add the remaining two wood chunks to the charcoal after the first hour. Add more lit briquettes as necessary to maintain a steady heat.

4 Meanwhile, in a large, nonreactive bowl whisk the remaining 3 tablespoons soy sauce, the remaining 3 tablespoons vinegar, the sugar, and the hot chili paste. Gradually whisk in the remaining ¼ cup canola oil and the sesame oil. Add the cabbage, peppers, and scallions and mix well. Cover and refrigerate for up to 1 hour before serving. Season with salt.

5 Remove the tofu from the smoker. Serve warm with the slaw.

THREE BEAN AND CHORIZO CHILI

PREP TIME: 20 minutes, plus about 55 minutes to simmer the chili

SPECIAL EQUIPMENT:
5-quart Dutch oven

SERVES: 6

8 ounces smoked chorizo sausage links, cut into ½-inch cubes
1 tablespoon extra-virgin olive oil
1 large yellow onion, finely chopped
1 large green bell pepper, cut into ½-inch dice
1 serrano *or* jalapeño chile pepper, seeded and minced
1 tablespoon minced garlic
3 tablespoons prepared chili powder
2 teaspoons ground cumin
2 teaspoons dried oregano
1 can (28 ounces) crushed tomatoes
1 bottle (12 fluid ounces) lager
2 cans (each 15 ounces) pinto beans, rinsed
1 can (15 ounces) red or pink beans, rinsed
1 can (15 ounces) garbanzo beans, rinsed
¾ teaspoon kosher salt
Sour cream (optional)
Grated cheddar cheese (optional)
Hot pepper sauce (optional)

1 In a 5-quart Dutch oven over medium heat, cook the chorizo with the oil until the chorizo begins to brown, about 5 minutes, stirring occasionally. Add the onion, bell pepper, chile pepper, and garlic. Cook until the onion is tender, about 5 minutes, stirring occasionally.

2 Add the chili powder, cumin, and oregano and stir for 15 seconds. Add the tomatoes and lager and stir well. Add all the beans and bring to a simmer. Reduce the heat to medium-low and simmer until the juices have thickened, about 45 minutes, stirring occasionally. Remove from the heat and season with the salt. Serve hot with sour cream, cheese, and hot pepper sauce, if desired.

This chili is an excellent side dish for the Barbecued Brisket Tamales (for the recipe, see page 73), but it can also be served as a main course.

CIDER AND BACON BEANS

IDEAL
GRILL:

PREP TIME: 15 minutes

COOKING TIME: about 1¼ hours

SPECIAL EQUIPMENT:
3-quart Dutch oven

SERVES: 8

3 cups fresh apple cider
3 tablespoons packed light brown sugar
⅓ cup ketchup
2 tablespoons spicy brown mustard
1 tablespoon Worcestershire sauce
4 slices bacon, cut into 1-inch pieces
1 large yellow onion, finely chopped
4 cans (each 15 ounces) white kidney (cannellini) beans, rinsed
  Kosher salt
  Ground black pepper

These beans are delicious on their own, but if you are a real smoke fanatic, smoke the beans with a wood that complements the bacon. For example, if you have used bacon smoked with apple wood, then use apple wood chips, or hickory wood chips for bacon that has been smoked with hickory.

1 Prepare the grill for direct and indirect cooking over low heat (250° to 350°F) (see pages 22–23).

2 In a medium saucepan over high heat, bring the cider to a boil. Cook until reduced to 1½ cups, about 10 minutes. Add the brown sugar, ketchup, mustard, and Worcestershire sauce and whisk until the sugar is dissolved. Set aside.

3 Place a 3-quart Dutch oven over DIRECT LOW HEAT, add the bacon and cook until crisp and browned, 10 to 12 minutes, stirring occasionally. Add the onion and cook until golden, 6 to 8 minutes, stirring occasionally. Add the beans and the cider mixture and stir well. Bring to a simmer. Slide the Dutch oven over INDIRECT LOW HEAT and cook, uncovered, with the grill lid closed, until the cooking liquid has reduced by about half, 45 to 50 minutes. Remove from the grill and let stand for about 5 minutes. Season with salt and pepper and serve warm.

ROASTED PEPPER MAC AND CHEESE

IDEAL
GRILL:

PREP TIME: 20 minutes

COOKING TIME: 30 to 42 minutes

SPECIAL EQUIPMENT:
5-quart Dutch oven

SERVES: 6 to 8

---

5   tablespoons plus 2 teaspoons
    unsalted butter, divided
4   poblano chile peppers
3   red bell peppers
⅓   cup all-purpose flour
3   cups whole milk, heated
4   cups grated sharp cheddar
    cheese, divided
1½ teaspoons kosher salt
½   teaspoon hot pepper sauce
1   pound dried elbow macaroni
2   large eggs

If poblano chile peppers are unavailable, use a bell pepper and a serrano or jalapeño chile pepper. Here's how: Seed and mince 1 large green bell pepper and 1 or 2 serrano or jalapeño chile peppers. In a small skillet over medium heat, warm 2 tablespoons extra-virgin olive oil. Sauté the peppers until tender, about 5 minutes, stirring occasionally. Stir into the sauce with the cheese.

1 Prepare the grill for direct and indirect cooking over medium heat (350° to 450°F) (see pages 22–23).

2 Grease a 5-quart Dutch oven with 2 teaspoons of the butter..

3 Brush the cooking grates clean. Grill all of the peppers over DIRECT MEDIUM HEAT, with the lid closed as much as possible, until blackened and blistered all over, 10 to 12 minutes, turning occasionally. Put the peppers in a bowl, cover with plastic wrap to trap the steam, and let stand for about 10 minutes. When cool enough to handle, remove and discard the stem ends, skin, and seeds. Cut into ½-inch dice.

4 In a large saucepan over medium-low heat, melt the remaining 5 tablespoons butter. Whisk in the flour and let bubble, without browning, for 1 minute. Whisk in the hot milk and bring to a simmer over medium heat, whisking often. Remove from the heat. Add 3½ cups of the cheese to the saucepan and stir until the cheese melts. Add the chopped peppers. Season with the salt and hot pepper sauce.

5 In a large saucepan of boiling, salted water cook the macaroni for about 3 minutes (it will be undercooked). Drain and return the macaroni to its saucepan.

6 In a medium bowl whisk the eggs. Gradually whisk in 1 cup of the hot cheese mixture, and then stir the egg mixture back into the saucepan. Pour over the macaroni and stir well. Spread in the prepared Dutch oven. Top with the remaining ½ cup cheese. Cook over INDIRECT MEDIUM HEAT, with the lid closed, until bubbling, 20 to 30 minutes. Remove from the grill and let rest for 5 minutes. Serve warm.

WARM POTATO AND BACON SALAD
WITH WHOLE-GRAIN MUSTARD DRESSING

PREP TIME: 30 minutes, plus about 25 minutes for the potatoes

SERVES: 6

Be sure to use waxy boiling potatoes with a thin, edible skin for this potato salad. They will hold together better than baking potatoes when tossed with the dressing.

3 pounds red potatoes, scrubbed
6 slices bacon, cut into 1-inch pieces
   Canola oil
¾ cup water
⅓ cup cider vinegar
2 tablespoons whole-grain mustard
1 tablespoon granulated sugar
   Kosher salt
   Ground black pepper
4 scallions, finely sliced, white and green parts separated
4 teaspoons all-purpose flour
2 tablespoons finely chopped fresh Italian parsley leaves

1 Put the potatoes in a large saucepan and cover with lightly salted water. Cover and bring to a boil over high heat. Reduce the heat to medium and set the saucepan lid ajar. Cook until the potatoes are just tender, about 25 minutes. Drain and rinse under cold running water. Set aside while making the dressing.

2 In a large skillet over medium heat, cook the bacon with 1 tablespoon oil until the bacon is crisp and browned, 8 to 10 minutes, stirring occasionally. Using a slotted spoon, transfer the bacon to a plate lined with paper towels. Measure the bacon fat: you should have 3 tablespoons. If not, add canola oil. Set the skillet aside.

3 In a small, nonreactive bowl whisk the water, vinegar, mustard, sugar, 1 teaspoon salt, and ¼ teaspoon pepper until the sugar and salt are dissolved. Set aside. Cut the potatoes into ¼-inch slices. Remove the potato skins, if desired.

4 Return the skillet with the bacon fat over medium heat. Add the white parts of the scallions and cook until wilted, about 2 minutes, stirring occasionally. Sprinkle with the flour and stir well. Whisk in the vinegar mixture and bring to a simmer. Reduce the heat to very low and simmer until the flour taste has disappeared, about 2 minutes. Remove from the heat and add the potato slices, bacon, the green parts of the scallions, and the parsley and toss gently to coat with the dressing. Season with salt and pepper. Serve warm.

FRESH CUCUMBER SALAD
WITH SOUR CREAM AND DILL DRESSING

PREP TIME: 15 minutes

DRAINING TIME: 1 to 3 hours

CHILLING TIME: at least 2 hours

SERVES: 6 to 8

4   large cucumbers, seeds removed,
     cut into ¼-inch half-moons
2¼ teaspoons kosher salt, divided
1   cup sour cream
3   tablespoons finely chopped fresh dill
3   tablespoons cider vinegar
1   teaspoon granulated sugar
¼   teaspoon ground black pepper
1   small red onion, thinly sliced

Use standard cucumbers for this salad. There is no advantage to using English cucumbers. In fact, this salad is a great way for using up a profusion of summer cucumbers.

Salt draws the excess water from the cucumbers and keeps them crisp in the dressing. Don't skip this step. Be sure to rinse the cucumber slices well to remove the salt before adding to the dressing.

1   In a colander toss the cucumbers with 2 teaspoons of the salt. Let stand in the sink to drain for at least 1 hour or up to 3 hours. Rinse well under cold running water and pat dry with paper towels.

2   In a medium, nonreactive bowl whisk the sour cream, dill, vinegar, sugar, the remaining ¼ teaspoon salt, and the pepper. Add the cucumbers and onion and mix well. Cover and refrigerate for at least 2 hours or up to 2 days. Serve chilled.

SWEET AND TANGY VEGETABLE SLAW

PREP TIME: **20 minutes**

CHILLING TIME: **about 2 hours**

SERVES: **8 to 10**

A food processor fitted with the slicing blade makes very quick work of preparing the cabbage, cucumber, onion, and peppers. Switch to the shredding blade for the carrots.

⅓ cup cider vinegar
⅓ cup canola oil
⅓ cup granulated sugar
1 tablespoon kosher salt
1½ teaspoons celery seed
½ teaspoon ground black pepper

6 cups thinly sliced green cabbage
1 English cucumber, cut into
    thin half-moons
2 cups shredded carrots
2 cups thinly sliced sweet yellow onion
1 cup thinly sliced red bell pepper
1 cup thinly sliced green bell pepper

1 In a large, nonreactive bowl whisk the vinegar, oil, sugar, salt, celery seed, and pepper until the sugar and salt are dissolved. Add all the vegetables and mix well. Cover and refrigerate until chilled, about 2 hours. To blend the flavors even more, you can refrigerate the slaw for up to 1 day.

2 Before serving, drain the slaw in a colander. Serve chilled.

Like most slaws, this one will wilt and the volume will decrease as the marinating time increases. If you like tender slaw, let it marinate overnight.

CLASSIC COLESLAW

PREP TIME: **15 minutes**

STANDING TIME: **30 minutes**

SERVES: **6**

1 head green cabbage, about 2 pounds,
thinly sliced
4 medium carrots, shredded
1 tablespoon kosher salt
⅔ cup mayonnaise
2 tablespoons sherry vinegar *or*
cider vinegar
1 tablespoon granulated sugar
1 tablespoon Dijon mustard
1 teaspoon ground black pepper

To avoid soggy coleslaw, remove as much water from the cabbage and carrots as you can. Do this by first salting the vegetables and letting them stand for 30 minutes. Then rinse the vegetables and squeeze them one handful at a time before adding the dressing.

1 In a large bowl toss the cabbage and carrots with the salt and let stand for 30 minutes.

2 Drain the cabbage and carrots in a colander and rinse well under cold running water. One handful at a time, squeeze the cabbage mixture to remove excess liquid and return to the bowl.

3 In a small bowl whisk the mayonnaise, vinegar, sugar, mustard, and pepper. Stir into the cabbage mixture. Serve right away.

GARLIC SPOON BREAD

IDEAL
GRILL:

PREP TIME: 20 minutes

COOKING TIME: about 35 minutes

SPECIAL EQUIPMENT:
10-inch cast-iron skillet

SERVES: 8

5 tablespoons unsalted butter, divided
1 tablespoon minced garlic
3 cups whole milk
1 teaspoon kosher salt
¼ teaspoon ground black pepper
1 cup stone-ground yellow cornmeal
⅔ cup grated sharp cheddar cheese
3 large eggs, separated, at
   room temperature

The easily adjusted, steady heat of a gas grill is best for cooking the spoon bread.

1 Prepare the grill for indirect cooking over medium heat (350° to 450°F) (see pages 22–23), keeping the temperature as close to 375°F as possible.

2 Grease a 10-inch cast-iron skillet with 1 tablespoon of the butter.

3 In a medium, heavy-bottomed saucepan over medium heat, melt 1 tablespoon of the remaining butter. Add the garlic and cook until it is softened but not browned, about 2 minutes, stirring often. Add the milk, salt, and pepper and bring to a simmer. Add the cornmeal and return to a simmer, whisking constantly. Reduce the heat to medium-low and simmer until very thick, about 2 minutes, whisking occasionally. Remove from the heat, add the remaining 3 tablespoons butter, and whisk until blended. Add the cheese and whisk until melted.

4 In a medium bowl beat the egg yolks. Gradually beat in ½ cup of the hot cornmeal mixture, and then stir the egg mixture back into the saucepan. In a medium bowl using an electric mixer set on high speed, beat the egg whites until soft peaks form. Stir about one-fourth of the egg whites into the cornmeal mixture, and then fold in the remaining egg whites with a rubber spatula. Spread in the prepared skillet.

5 Grill over INDIRECT MEDIUM HEAT, with the lid closed, until the spoon bread has puffed evenly and is golden brown, about 35 minutes. Remove from the grill and serve right away.

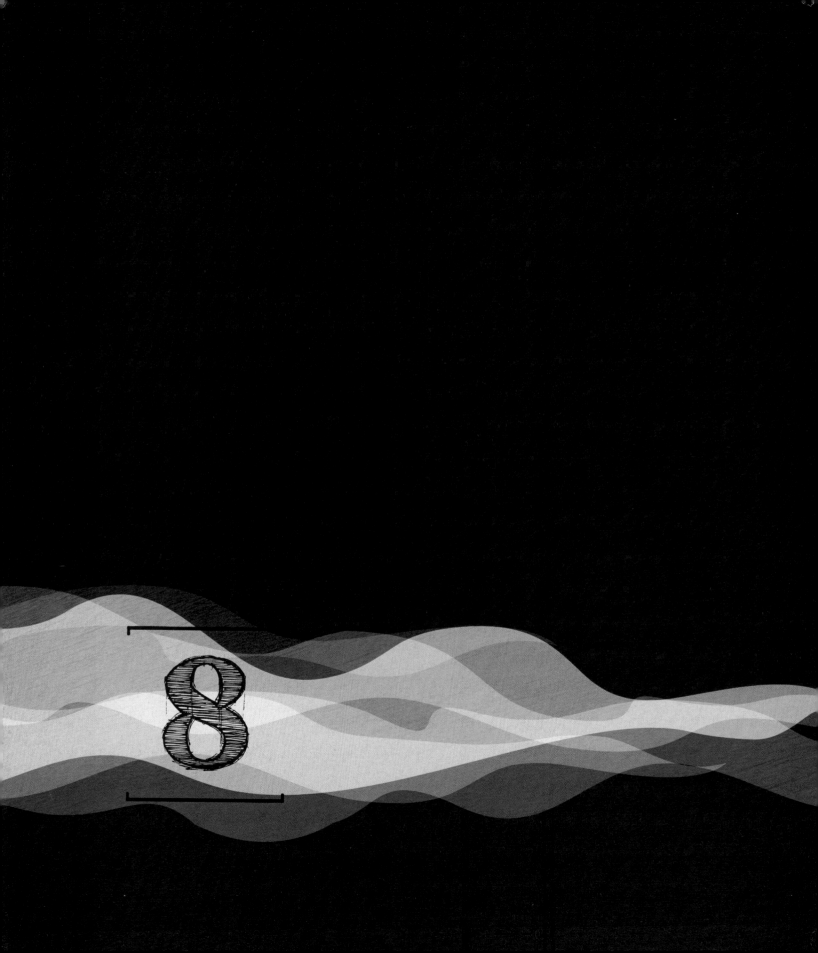

Resources

SAFETY

GRILL SAFETY

Please read your owner's guide and familiarize yourself with and follow all "dangers," "warnings," and "cautions." Also follow the grilling procedures and maintenance requirements listed in your owner's guide.

If you cannot locate the owner's guide for your grill model, please contact the manufacturer prior to use. If you have any questions concerning the "dangers," "warnings," and "cautions" contained in your Weber® gas or charcoal grill owner's guide, or if you do not have an owner's guide for your specific grill model, please contact Weber-Stephen Products LLC Customer Service at 1.800.446.1071 before using your grill. You can also access your owner's guide online at www.weber.com.

BASIC FOOD SAFETY

Follow these basic rules to make sure your meal is as safe as it is tasty:

1 **AVOID THE "DANGER ZONE."** If meat sits between 40°F and 140°F ("the danger zone") for too long, unwelcome bacteria start to grow. So don't let it sit out on the counter for extended periods of time— 20 minutes is fine; two hours is not. And after dinner, don't let smoked meat sit out on the table for hours. Wrap it up and refrigerate it. Besides, leftovers are among smoking's best rewards.

2 **WASH AND CLEAN ANYTHING THAT TOUCHED RAW MEAT.** Never set a cooked piece of meat back on a cutting board that held it raw without first washing it with soap and hot water. The same goes for knives, tongs, and other tools.

3 **NEVER USE A MEAT MARINADE RIGHT AWAY AS A SAUCE.** Pour the marinade into a saucepan and bring to a boil before you serve it to anyone. This will kill any harmful bacteria.

4 **THAW FROZEN MEAT SLOWLY IN THE REFRIGERATOR.** It's also safe to thaw meat in cold water (which is faster), provided that you seal the meat in a plastic bag, you submerge the bag in cold water, and you change the water every hour. Don't let the water get above 40°F.

5 **SHARPEN YOUR KNIVES.** Dull knives are much more dangerous than sharp knives because they force you to apply too much pressure, which can lead to slips and cuts. So get a sharpening steel and use it at least once a week.

6 **REMEMBER THAT RECIPE TIMES ARE SUGGESTIONS, NOT GUARANTEES.** Your smoker may be a little hotter than mine. The roast from my fridge may have been a little cooler than yours. Mine was thicker, but yours weighed more. You may be smoking at a higher altitude than I am. All these things affect timing, so use the recipes as guides, but then verify the desired doneness by inserting an instant-read thermometer into the center of the meat, not touching a bone.

USDA AND CHEF STANDARDS FOR DONENESS

For optimal safety, the United States Department of Agriculture (USDA) recommends cooking red meat to 145°F (final temperature) and ground red meat to 160°F. The USDA believes that 145°F is medium rare, but virtually all chefs today believe medium rare is closer to 130°F. The chart at right compares chef standards with USDA recommendations. Ultimately, doneness decisions are your choice.

DONENESS	CHEF STANDARDS	USDA
RED MEAT: Rare	120° to 125°F	n/a
RED MEAT: Medium rare	125° to 135°F	145°F
RED MEAT: Medium	135° to 145°F	160°F
RED MEAT: Medium well	145° to 155°F	n/a
RED MEAT: Well done	155°F +	170°F
PORK	145° to 150°F	145° to 160°F
POULTRY	160° to 165°F	165°F

METRIC EQUIVALENTS

METRIC EQUIVALENTS FOR DIFFERENT TYPES OF INGREDIENTS

A standard cup measure of a dry or solid ingredient will vary in weight depending on the type of ingredient. A standard cup of liquid is the same volume for any type of liquid. Use the following chart when converting standard cup measures to grams (weight) or milliliters (volume).

STANDARD CUP	FINE POWDER (e.g. flour)	GRAIN (e.g. rice)	GRANULAR (e.g. sugar)	LIQUID SOLIDS (e.g. butter)	LIQUID (e.g. milk)
⅛	18 grams	19 grams	24 grams	25 grams	30 milliliters
¼	35 grams	38 grams	48 grams	50 grams	60 milliliters
⅓	47 grams	50 grams	63 grams	67 grams	80 milliliters
½	70 grams	75 grams	95 grams	100 grams	120 milliliters
⅔	93 grams	100 grams	125 grams	133 grams	160 milliliters
¾	105 grams	113 grams	143 grams	150 grams	180 milliliters
1	140 grams	150 grams	190 grams	200 grams	240 milliliters

USEFUL EQUIVALENTS FOR LIQUID INGREDIENTS BY VOLUME

¼ teaspoon				=	1 milliliter	
½ teaspoon				=	2 milliliters	
1 teaspoon				=	5 milliliters	
3 teaspoons =	1 tablespoon		= ½ fluid ounce	=	15 milliliters	
	2 tablespoons	= ⅛ cup	= 1 fluid ounce	=	30 milliliters	
	4 tablespoons	= ¼ cup	= 2 fluid ounces	=	60 milliliters	
	5⅓ tablespoons	= ⅓ cup	= 3 fluid ounces	=	80 milliliters	
	8 tablespoons	= ½ cup	= 4 fluid ounces	=	120 milliliters	
	10⅔ tablespoons	= ⅔ cup	= 5 fluid ounces	=	160 milliliters	
	12 tablespoons	= ¾ cup	= 6 fluid ounces	=	180 milliliters	
	16 tablespoons	= 1 cup	= 8 fluid ounces	=	240 milliliters	
	1 pint	= 2 cups	= 16 fluid ounces	=	480 milliliters	
	1 quart	= 4 cups	= 32 fluid ounces	=	960 milliliters	
			33 fluid ounces	=	1000 milliliters	= 1 liter

USEFUL EQUIVALENTS FOR DRY INGREDIENTS BY WEIGHT

To convert ounces to grams, multiply the number of ounces by 30.

1 ounce	=	¹⁄₁₆ pound	=	30 grams
4 ounces	=	¼ pound	=	120 grams
8 ounces	=	½ pound	=	240 grams
12 ounces	=	¾ pound	=	360 grams
16 ounces	=	1 pound	=	480 grams

USEFUL EQUIVALENTS FOR LENGTH

To convert inches to centimeters, multiply the number of inches by 2.5.

1 inch	= 2.5 centimeters
6 inches = ½ foot	= 15 centimeters
12 inches = 1 foot	= 30 centimeters
36 inches = 3 feet = 1 yard	= 90 centimeters
40 inches	= 100 centimeters = 1 meter

USEFUL EQUIVALENTS FOR COOKING/OVEN TEMPERATURES

	FAHRENHEIT	CELSIUS	GAS MARK
Freezing point	32°F	0°C	
Room temperature	68°F	20°C	
Boiling point	212°F	100°C	
Bake	325°F	160°C	3
	350°F	180°C	4
	375°F	190°C	5
	400°F	200°C	6
	425°F	220°C	7
	450°F	230°C	8

INDEX

INDEX

AUTHOR	Jamie Purviance
MANAGING EDITOR	Marsha Capen
PHOTOGRAPHY	Tim Turner, Photographer and Photo Art Direction Takamasa Ota, Digital Guru Christy Clow, Photo Assistant Michael Anton Herbert, Photo Assistant
FOOD STYLING	Lynn Gagné, Food Stylist Nina Albazi, Assistant Food Stylist
COLOR IMAGING AND IN-HOUSE PREPRESS	Weber Creative Services
CONTRIBUTORS	April Cooper, Sarah Epstein, Mary Goodbody, Norbert Kempinger, Kevin Kolman, Rick Rodgers, Mark Scarbrough, Edna Schlosser, Corinne Trang, Bruce Weinstein, Terri Wuerthner
DESIGN AND PRODUCTION	rabble+rouser, inc.: Christina Schroeder, Chief Rouser Marsha Capen, Editorial Director Shum Prats, Creative Director Elaine Chow, Art Director Abby Wilson, Assistant Editor
ILLUSTRATIONS	Keith Witmer
INDEXER	Becky LaBrum
WEBER-STEPHEN PRODUCTS LLC	Mike Kempster, Chief Marketing Officer Brooke Jones, Director of Marketing
ROUND MOUNTAIN MEDIA	Susan Maruyama, Consulting Publishing Director
OXMOOR HOUSE	Jim Childs, Vice President and Publishing Director Fonda Hitchcock, Brand Manager

10 9 8 7 6 5 4 3 2 1

ISBN-10: 0-376-02067-9
ISBN-13: 978-0-376-02067-3
Library of Congress Control Number: 2011943987

Weber Customer Service: 1.800.446.1071

www.weber.com®
www.sunset.com
www.oxmoorhouse.com
www.rabbleandrouser.com

YOUR THOUGHTS